"THAT WHICH ONCE WAS YOUR GREATEST SHADOW WILL ONE DAY BECOME YOUR GREATEST GIFT."

UNLEASH THE BEAST
127 thoughts on self mastery

Self-published edition
ISBN: 978-0-473-39948-1

All rights reserved
Copyright © 2017

Written, designed and illustrated by
Polina Outkina

www.polinaoutkina.com

.....

Get the divination deck

Contents

0	Peace	10	
1	Energy	11	
2	Being	12	
3	Lull	13	
4	Clarity	14	
5	Imprint	15	
6	Identity	16	
7	Presence	17	
8	Health	18	
9	Awakening	19	
10	Unity	20	
11	Release	22	
12	Flow	23	
13	Time	24	
14	Sadness	25	
15	Heart	26	
16	Embodiment	27	
17	Vibration	28	
18	Shedding	32	
19	Independence	33	
20	Lack	34	
21	Pace	35	
22	Selfishness	36	
23	Start	37	
24	Ambition	38	
25	The Dream	40	
26	Thought	41	
27	Thoughtlessness	42	
28	Humour	43	
29	Laughter	44	
30	Competition	45	
31	Negativity	46	
32	Chaos	47	
33	Survival	48	
34	Ageing	49	
35	Regeneration	50	
36	Fatigue	52	
37	Trouble	53	
38	Unsuccessful	54	
39	Independence	55	
40	Fearfulness	58	
41	Resonance	59	
42	Pride	60	
43	Success	61	
44	Death	62	
45	Enjoyment	63	
46	BE!!	64	
47	Beauty	64	
48	Stillness	65	
49	Grace	66	
50	Solitude	67	
51	Depression	68	
52	Dis-ease	69	
53	Prickliness	70	
54	Resistance	70	
55	Stagnancy	71	
56	Crossroads	73	
57	Worries	74	
58	Destruction	74	
59	Compulsion	75	
60	Rage	76	
61	Passion	77	
62	Fragmentation	78	
63	Entities	80	

64 Authenticity	81	96 Privilege	116
65 Illness	82	97 Needs	117
66 Mastery	84	98 Inner Value	117
67 Progress	84	99 Mischief	118
68 Inversion	85	100 Money	120
69 Universe	86	101 Greed	120
70 Human	87	102 Manifestation	122
71 Inspiration	88	103 Silliness	124
72 Impulse	89	104 Captivity	125
73 Conditions	90	105 Materialism	126
74 Self Belief	91	106 Expenses	127
75 False Intension	92	107 Habits	128
76 Miracle	96	108 Dependency	129
77 Illusion	97	109 Unleashing	130
78 False Value	98	110 Beastliness	132
79 Attachment	99	111 Insanity	133
80 Entwining	100	112 The Shift	134
81 Expiry	101	113 Unconsciousness	135
82 Bliss	103	114 Prayer	136
83 Rebirth	104	115 The Chosen	138
84 Freshness	105	116 Revolution	139
85 Conclusion	105	117 Freakishness	140
86 Growth	106	118 The Beast	141
87 Perseverance	108	119 Transformation	144
88 Primitiveness	109	120 Power	145
89 Fiction	110	121 Mutation	147
90 Perfection	111	122 Shame	148
91 Recovery	112	123 Phenomenon	149
92 Determination	113	124 Sabotage	150
93 Servicing	113	125 Separation	152
94 Status	114	126 Trust	153
95 Pedestal	115	127 Welcome	154

This is an unleashed little book.

An epic little book free to experience this world in it's own right without censorship, fear, spiritual context or need to appeal. This book is a being in itself now – a free one that is able to be whatever it wants and yes – here in your hands – it is able to be of service and yet still remain itself. However it affects you or however it interacts with you is it's business entirely. From either it came and perhaps to either it will one day return. This book is free to roam as it may please. It is in itself a being.

This little book was conceived and sculpted in two hours one ecstatic morning after showing up in one of my dreams. This book is collection of DNA truths that came to me itself. I didn't fathom it neither did I summon it. It just crystalized itself completely as it wanted to be. This book is a product of a journey through the abyss of collective human psyche. It is about the unspeakable, the unseen, the silent, the lost and yes – the leashed. This book was a process of self finding. Each lost word tumbling freely out of my depths and into the light where they are now turning their own little vortex of creation.

This book is freedom or liberation of one's own worries and depths. It is as meaningless as it is meaningful – a block of 127 thoughts that lead me to victory over my disconnection with shadow and helped me to integrate myself into something else - something yet unseen – the fuller more empowered free flowing version of myself. The process of writing this book has helped me to heal my void between self and the self I thought I didn't want to be. It mended the bridges between shadow and light and we know to be able to create freely one must do that – one must create wholeness without superficiality or judgement within. That is what adult hood is about. It is about merging shadow and light into union where they can along each other create in peace.

Though this book is not absolute, purely worded or perfect in it's execution it is a tool that helped me through it's creation and I hope that it heals you too. The rough nature of it is what makes it itself – free or at least able to shift within it's own meanings and parables.

This is not a book of pain though it talks about pain. It is not a book of wants or needs though it does talk about them too. It is not a book about service though as you are reading it it is of service to you. It is not a book to become whole though whole you may become quicker through understanding it's concepts. This is not a very special or surprising book either. It is just itself - a book that I wrote when I was drunk on life and it's outcomes.

Hopefully that through reading it, you create for yourself a new portal into your shadow and through this portal create liberation of it too. Liberate through integration not through self rejection. Balance your shadow. Balance yourself. Read the book already! It's waiting for you :D

With Gratitude

Polina Outkina

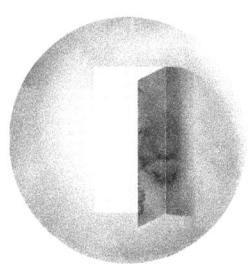

"YOU ARE THE DOOR TO YOUR FREEDOM"

$$\frac{O}{\text{Peace}}$$

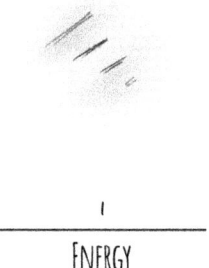

Energy

Everything is energy.

Life doesn't provide many opportunities if you are not coping energetically. This is the quantum truth and forever will be. It is at the basis of all creation. Energy is the master navigator, the sustainer, the physical employer, the builder and the voice of your life! It is what is behind and in front of the curtain on this great stage of creation as it unfolds. If you aren't coping in your current of energy grid, you are not anywhere - because you are not truly within you! If you aren't able to be deeply you then where are you? Nowhere.

Energy. You are energy. It is also important to energize as it through it, to sustain yourself with plenty of it, follow it, replenish with it in the way that is best suited to the moment, become more of it, circulate more of it, and vibrate it as far as you can go! There is no use in becoming like anyone else's energy, becoming the energy of your ancestors or any other figures you feel are stronger or brighter than you. You cannot. Energy doesn't imprint or stand still forever as a taster of itself or a sample. It can never stay neutral. Although all is one, the unique energy bouquet of you has to be sustained exactly as itself through all the shifts that the collective energy of the world undergoes.

Energy cannot be taken. Only circulated. You cannot harvest energy organically by pulling on anything which doesn't come easy. Energy stunts when you are trying and trying. As it cannot be pulled, it cannot be pushed without imbalance. You cannot start it up like a motor where it will not flourish itself. You cannot spark it with a place, a job, an idea or a vacation if there is no true feeling within it. You cannot even ask for it or reap it from God as the master energy. Energy is simply yours and within you already – it is your voice and your truth. It is up to you what you choose to do with it. The more truthful you are to your energy and your own life the more this energy will spark up and get you through. As you invert into your own source feeling, your own unique energy and divinity – you are energized and your energy multiplies.

Your energy is yours. Own it. Own yourself.

Hurdles, punches of life, all is easily shed and seen as soon as you are in your energy zone, so do that! Be you. Become that which you are more and more and you will increase in energy. Become less affiliated with that which is you and the energy will wane. That's the way it is and the way forward to all peaks and crevices of your life. Enjoy it as you trace yourself through the valleys and the mountains of your very special life.

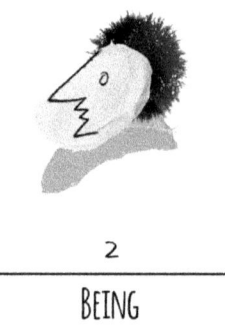

2
BEING

Be yourself. Be you just as you are, right now!

You have no need to be another person, a muted version of who you think you might be or anyone else's person of significance. You have no need to be any body that is not you inside your body right now. Be yourself and that will guide you through all torment and troubles in life as soon as you start doing what you're meant to do and that is: Just Be You!

It is not hard. What do you create for yourself if you think it's hard? You think as if you are not yourself. If you yourself are against you - you do not believe in you. So do not think hard about this. It is simple

You are enough.

You don't need a job, a place or a calling. You just need you to be you – that is the main reason of why you've come here. You are here because you wanted to be you – not for a job a person or a purpose. Just for fun!

Start advertising what you are inside to other people, to your loved ones, to yourself. Show it. Start understanding deeper with each moment what you are comfortable as yourself, inside yourself. If nobody listens to you, that's not so bad. Stop trying to get other people to know you better than you know yourself. That is futile. Just listen to you and be your own best friend. Right now, as you are now embodied!

3
Lull

"In the mean time": between jobs, between partners and between things - you might think you're at a lull. It is not a lull. It is a peak, for you are here with just you, it is all you will ever need! If you have got some luck, you are able to be alone within. When nobody else notices, you get to become you more and more, and as you do that, you are able to create the greater being of you.

Every lull between adventures is a hidden peak – learn to love it!

This mentality of having to loose or win is the worst one yet. Competitive mentality has been dividing this world for a long time now. There is no need to be this or that for any reason. You are you - already you. You are not alone, never were. You have no true deep need to become anything that fits any other social or economic mould. You have nothing already no matter where you are from. You are ether and a figment of the imagination… or rather THE imagination of God! Be it here.

> "BECOME THAT WHICH YOU ARE MORE AND MORE AND YOU WILL INCREASE IN ENERGY"

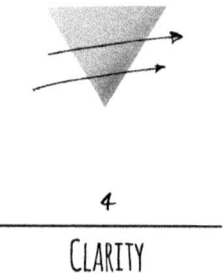

4
CLARITY

Unclear? "Aren't we all?" – you might think.

You have no need to be here, where you are (literally) if you are thinking "where is my purpose?" You might as well fade into the ether again, fall through the ground or "poof!" Disappear!

If you are here, you must remember that you aren't guaranteed a thing my dear. You are nothing but you and truly have nothing but you at all. The only thing that is guaranteed is that you are here - so start being here. That is truly your only task.

We all can find the way forward with clarity. Clarity is simple. It is in each breath and in each step. You just have to walk towards who you are, not away from you. Stop trying to walk towards a job or a partnership, it is illusionary such a walk, as it is unconscious. The mirage will be taken away when the time comes. Offcourse, to be under the tide is to be on top of the tide - our problems are illusionary. There is no condition with life, you create them with crooked thinking if you do think something is true or you feel it is compatible with greater schemes of life beyond your joy. That's tough.

Stop thinking: "am I at a win or at a loss here?" No comparison. The body is wired to know itself, not your thoughts. Thoughts of better or worse are a false presence without which you can do....and will do better! Walk towards that which your body pulls towards not out of "I don't know".

Are you clear? Do you think straight?

If you are watching your life and your experiences, thinking "where is it going?", "where are these thoughts trailing?", you're not thinking straight. After this book or at any moment through it, please put down all books and recycled thought forms. Start thinking straight in all clarity. Wake up. Walk your own special walk even though you might not yet know where it all leads.

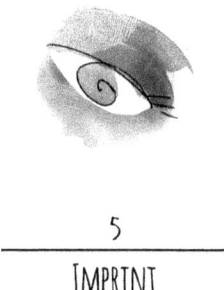

5
Imprint

Everything is malleable, all is equally dangerous as all is beautiful. Things imprint, everything changes every day and yes, all beings imprint each other's worlds all the time. Let it fold. Don't cling to any concepts.

There is no need to push anything in front of you like dinner in front of a prised dog or a line of cocaine in front of a nose in order to get your concepts straight. No more indoctrination or mental pollution that you never needed. Do not put fake enrichment in front of you in order to get yourself forward: newspapers, books, "knowledge", magazines, work… No. You are not that. You know more than enough in being who you are – a living, breathing human.

You do not need to read any doctrine or take part in anyone's concepts if they distract you from your just BEING here. For that reason, stop this book here if you can – if you are strong and you know your worth. However, if you are still curious in seeing what I come up with next, well, I'll be your friend and companion in the next phase of your life then…. why….? Imprinting.

All things cling. All things imprint each other constantly. With just a little bit of attention – you have something permanently grooved into reality. Your Facebook page clings to you like nothing else. If you are clinging to a computer screen - it becomes you. If you cling to a friend, they become you and share your experiences even when you are not there. Be weary of your choices.

Start thinking straight – what am I clinging to and what or who is currently programing me? Why am I here and what am I wasting my time on? Start listening to yourself and stop identifying through other people's thoughts and feelings. Be one with all things but do not fixate. Release and be loose with all creation. This is not about anger, stereotypes or pointing of fingers. Just understand: your environment and your choices make you. Make appropriate changes if you care to. Find your strength of impression within you on the world. Find your own special stream of consciousness. Act now.

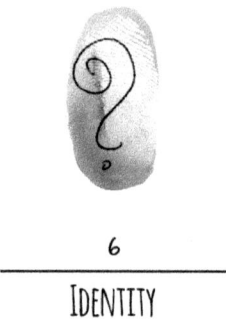

6
IDENTITY

Do not identify in relationship to anything or anyone. Comparison of yourself or creation of separate identities for yourself depending on occasion is bad, very bad. It is both distorting and futile to twist yourself in order to falsely identify or in order to politely find compromise and thus be in a "good place in your life".

In conditional filtering of ourselves, we create a false identity that automatically ties to a cause that is not sovereign. Residue away false selves, let them fall off like old autumn leaves – whoever you created yourself into for others or for your ego self. Even if these identities are well mastered or seem well oiled – even if you just want to be somebody else's hero or a "good person" - All inorganic identity is a hindrance in your life for it is a twisted way for your energy to flow through you. In false identity one is breached and distorted, generating much less power and abundance on all levels. Release false identities. Breathe.

The box you are creating for yourself through any polite or false response is real and will make you suffer as the walls close in tighter with each repetition of a false formula. Re-identify as soon as you understand that what you have in the making is not yours! Don't be afraid of inconsistent swings of trajectories. Find your super self now to the best of your understanding yet. Let all constructs polite and otherwise drop off like autumn leaves.

Start feeling. Start enriching through your own physical being. Be your own, be with pride and with strength. Do not care who is in front of you or who is behind you. Create consistency in yourself to be that in all circumstance for it makes you powerful fully, wholesomely, honestly. Sustainable power radiates from inner truth always.

Start worshiping your own presence NOW. It is you and your only truth.

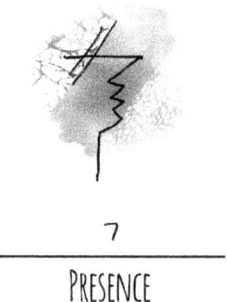

7
Presence

Your presence? Well, "The Presence" is truly all of us.

If you are concerned about having a presence in people's lives, forget it, you're doing it wrong. If you are not present, you are "not" – you are not present within yourself, which is the most potent point of reference. Presence cannot be measured or understood through any other than you. It is within yourself – it is yours alone to perceive as you do.

You cannot find it in conversation, nor perceive it through attraction or magnetism. Effect on others isn't presence. It's opportunity to mend together or to startle enough to change a story about you and them, but it isn't real presence. It is smoke and mirrors to an extent and partially natural chemistry.

True presence is something that is yours and forever will be so. It is with you everywhere. In the dark, in the light, it persists and it is always available no matter the setting or experience. It cannot be found in any virtue that is placed upon a pedestal, neither can it be tweaked, manipulated or created. It is just yours as you remain present inside. If you are someone looking around for your worth or what it is that is needed in the world, where you are applicable or what you can give or represent – your presence is lost. It disappears.

Build yourself from the inside in. Start fresh. A fresh new possibility of a fresh new feeling of you.

A glowing presence without deceit relies on inner core and stamina. A healthy resonance towards greater vitality is needed for greater energetic capability and a fun filled life. In health and stamina presence radiates, in dis-ease deceitful presence is created. In conscious activation of greater health and a drawing of everything that is vital and beautiful in we drain out all intensity and create ease. Through beauty we flow, through darkness we fold.

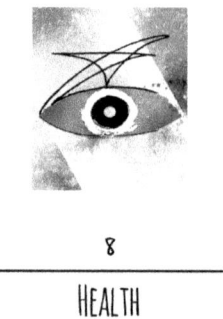

8

HEALTH

Health is personal freedom. It expands, shifts and recreates itself with time to aid one's spectrum of experience, allowing one to power through life with grace and strength. To catch up and to catch on we must constantly work wonders inside of ourselves to shift ourselves more fully into the new energies and accommodate our ever changing bodies.

Health is the sexiest thing on this planet.

You get a body and you get to use it like a pro from the day you are born. If there is tiredness accompanying the body or if it is challenging to commit to the simplest of actions like sitting or standing, you're not doing well. There is need for realignment and perhaps some vital amusement!

You are you. This body is no joke. It is you completely.

Some may say "I am not my body". But yes, you are your body. The body that is yours is what you vibrate as, it is exceptional as it is the most articulate, accurate description of your soul and the specific human path that you are to take this time. It is not a myth nor is it a mirage. It is the mirror of you. There is no other body for the special path that you are treading. Yes, this body is currently the only you, all speculation and over-souls aside. Own it! there is no other you in any other dimension be it digital, physical, conceptual, intergalactic or ethereal. This body is it. You are right here, right now. You belong here and this is where you should be: whole, complete and thriving inwardly and offcourse outwardly. Your outward world is an exact mirror of your inward world through space and time. There is no question.

To be born here means to conform to this reality and your body – to let it do it's natural human thing - the walk thing, the embodied thing, the feeling breathing and sensing thing. Awaken yourself within your physicality first as it is the given, before all other dimensions become available with ease. Don't wonder too far out there into the ether if you do not know your natural human form yet. Be it – what you are made to be naturally, learn from the everyday phenomena of your body, become enlightened fast.

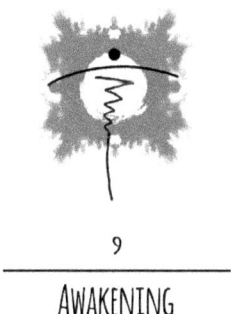

9

Awakening

As you become more yourself inside, you wake up to the outer world around you. We are one being. Stop hiding! We already know. We already trust and love you dearly. We are you. We are one. We all perceive you beyond what you would wish to hide. Start recognising this and be at peace.

We all see, hear and smell you half a globe away though we wouldn't think it as we are "Not supposed to" notice. Such is the veil here on this planet for now. We are all one and though we cannot express it fully, we do however all remember this inside our unconscious mind. Each one of us, each fibre of our beings.

Forget all forgery: the make of your appearance, the social media charade, the status of your job, the plastic smiles in those family photos - we all see each other. Although the world of physical illusion is deceiving, you are still energetically perceived exactly as you are which cannot be denied. We can all understand and see you…and even curate your life for you in the secrecy of our souls. We all know you very well.

There are no lies possible in this constantly evolving universe. A body is a body. You're just you. There is no need to hide. All is awake. We are aware of you. Drop your unconscious need to be forgiven, stop your hiding of yourself, your skin, your insecurities. We can all see everything – you are one with us already – in the best you and the worst you. Nothing is missed, nothing is made fault either.

"WE ALL KNOW YOU VERY WELL. WE ARE ONE."

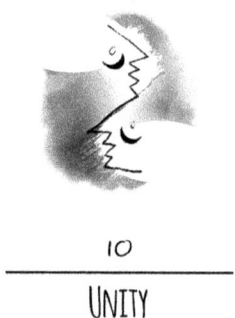

10
UNITY

Everyone feels everything. This is for all of us with no exception. Acute sensitivity isn't a factor. We are all united in our consciousness. Information travels freely between realms both physical and ethereal. There is no space and time my friend so we are yes, virtually unlimited in our perception. We are all seeing all knowing, and offcourse you are too.

Don't starve yourself or your body of any truths, don't lie or a lie you will become. Lie is a Band-Aid and will not organically exist without failure, as this universe will not support it. With time if lie becomes the way of life, superficial band aids grow upon each other and become parts of you too. Because there is humour in that which is false too, it is easy to become unlovable to oneself if Band-Aid choices are regular ones. Unity is hard to find or fathom then but choices always exist.

If disassociation from unity of all things has been a way of life for long, that is alright too, we are all needed here no matter how far off the track we go. That which is false isn't hard to shed in a need for unity. Unity isn't something that is gained, it is something that is already there waiting when we release that which is false.

> "WE ARE ALL SEEING, ALL KNOWING, AND OFCOURSE, YOU ARE TOO."

II
Release

What have you got in that closet? What is in there - in your heart, stomach or brain? Throw it away if it is hard to see. Keep throwing away whatever you do not need and do not really care for or else you become what is not you more and more with time. You loose parts of your soul that way. Parts of your heart. Parts of you. Don't attach to anything for it imprints and curbs the soul into distorted view of itself. You are you. That is that.

Because you are free, born naked and sovereign to this simple planet, you have to understand what freedom is truth and It is very simple. "Freedom's just another word for nothing left to loose." (Janis Joplin) The less you have the more endowed you are in other ways. Energy replenishes and makes sense in new ways as what is lost or given is replenished anew with greater force and strength.

Energy flows, all is as liquid. It doesn't bunch and doesn't wait for a rainy day like money in a bank account - energy moves freely, balances and creates itself in new powerful ways always upgrading it's states. Therefor - it cannot be gathered consciously. No need for old ideas, feelings and conversations – let it go. Recycle the old into new possibilities. An emptiness is always fulfilled in a creative space of heart with no clutter.

"FREE YOURSELF. EXPLORE MORE!"

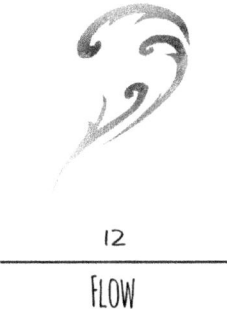

12
Flow

If it's not flowing – there is blockage - let it go!

If you aren't slowed down by a message, don't read it. If you aren't slowed down by a person, don't make it your priority to slow down for them. Your inner mechanisms are always ticking knowing what you need when you need it, so, if it's not somehow magically pulling you into a new vortex, leave it be. If it isn't flowing through you completely - let it go.

Each step is reality formative. The gift of your time and attention is permanent. Yours is a program building gaze in a program built universe. So as you attend to something, you embed it. You make it more plausible, more alive and more real.

Allow yourself to be program free sometimes. Flow through your life. Just be yourself as if a child in great simplicity and inner silence. Don't stop for anything or anybody unless you are so peaked and perked by this experience that you can't handle the tension - you have to follow through and learn more. If you want it – connect to it. But only if you organically feel to.

Natural curiosity in the natural flow of things is active energy. Use the energy of magic and interest to create a much larger creation scheme for your life. If the feeling is clear, have a look and follow it. You won't be disappointed.

If it is hard to define or you have a lot on your plate, time to unclutter before you voyage.

If you are encumbered, you won't let yourself encounter magic in all it's love and simplicity. As you become less clustered by things you do not need to create or experience or become – natural curiosity creates new moods and possibilities, along with other beings and people wanting to play. This is the best use of time. If you do not feel enticed, do not waste your time as you do not have a lot of room for exploration perhaps due to over encumbering yourself. Free yourself = explore more. But, if it is hard to generate interest for life – perhaps time has to be addressed as a concept.

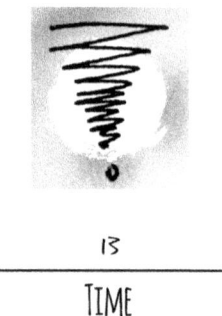

13

TIME

Time - as paper or any other kind of matter – imprintable. However, it is also unlike matter in the way that it is lucid and infinite. It spills, stretches and distorts - making it truly immeasurable. Like a morphing fabric, time creates a pattern of energy and mirage that we have programmed ourselves using it's unique structure.

In every day circumstance, we all give away our time unconsciously often and that is not a good thing, but we don't need to worry. Even though you already wasted and do waste a lot of time reading this little book of mine, and surely I may have done writing it, you need to understand that time is not something that is negative or oppressive, neither is it an important mathematic guideline to your life. Time is potentially a welcome, ageless friend who knows how to skip rope!

Time naturally morphs and shifts more than we'd like to admit with the power of our thoughts and emotions. As you master your moment – your true "now", you will just get on with it and jump time like skipping rope! Time is untameable for those who abide to it. For those who are open to change and receive – time is not a structure - It is a programming tool for one's own unique matrix.

Your capacity of manifestation and experience does fill up fast. You do not need half at least of what you think: what you think you should see, do, work, achieve, understand, spend time with, believe, experience and so on. Your time might be short because of that need to fill it up with things you don't yet have the capacity to truly involve in (hence why they are hard to achieve or aren't really available yet). So switch it up. Enjoy what you have now – absorb it in simple ways and time will stretch and allow more change.

Time morphs as you learn to play with it like a kid. Time is tough if you let it be your guide upon which you build your world.

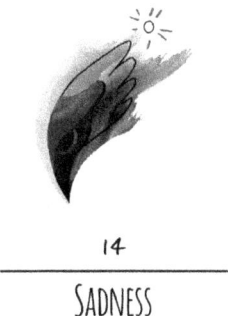

14
Sadness

This is the biggest hindrance for everybody on this planet really. You may also think you are not fine, not ok. It is not unusual here.

Are you delusional? Yes, you are likely to be delusional if you need a self help book, or if you're spending time writing one. If you feel that it's important to sow seeds slowly, to start slowing down – to become somebody of value to yourself or others…you aren't fine. You are sad.

Is the act of becoming an issue here? Is it tough to face yourself? What are you? Are you a child or an elderly person? If you are neither too young or too old the nature of becoming isn't an issue. You are. Just are.

Don't delude yourself.

There is delusion in the air if you feel you need help to "be better" while doing little about it yourself through your own personal experience or expression serendipitously. If you think you need to give your time away to any practice, preacher or situation, it's all part of it – the sadness. So stop wasting your time and find your own heart beat. Now. It has all you will ever need!

"NOBODY HAS A HEART QUITE LIKE YOURS"

15
HEART

Step to the rhythm of your own drum! That's right, you have one that is just perfect for you and it is always just right on cue. It is your heart offcourse, what else?

You have a watch? A playlist? A favourite piece of music that defines you? That's not your rhythm. You can't measure you – a shape shifting organic unique and powerful being with anything capsulated or inorganic! So stop connecting to the rhythms around you that do not have your moment, your vibe, your heart. Nobody has the keys to your unique rhythm. Nobody has a heart quite like yours.

Yes, time is a constant phenomenon here for most people, yet it is not constant or truly measurable in it's illusion. There is no true scale of time as it's an illusionary little trick of life for you and I to measure up to if we silly enough to live by the clock. Throw out your clocks and watches. Step to your own beat.

Live by your spirit! It's timed perfectly to all events on this planet and all things that are happening right around you. Each frequency – your heart understands and reflects perfectly. It is prepared for all that is already programmed and that which is still surprising and untameable. All the off beats, all the ups and downs – you heart knows it all entirely, deeply and profoundly. Surrender to it.

Supreme measure and timing of all things lives inside your very heart. All things reside there, all matter and all force. If you can't feel the safety and the know how of your heart – you're out of luck. You need to find it inside again – the beat, the voice within that guarantees the best outcome to be had. It knows what to do every time and what the next steps are way before the mind can even glimpse it. When you find it again – the beat of you - let it move you. Let it bounce with you, let it be your signature, your story told and yet untold too. The written letter to yourself and all the stuff between the lines too. That's your inner magic.

Concentrate inside on it – the beat and the balance of your heart, the voice of God and the centre of your torus – "energy mind". Feel it and in time - it'll become natural to be in it. Just this, just you, just true to each moment independently and freely. Within.

16
EMBODIMENT

Reader! Be yourself already! Yes, that's right. Yourself. Be you and do what you love!

You had that dream? You are here to become it! Doesn't matter how far out it is or how far away you feel from it sometimes. You are here. This is all you get – just do it!

Did you want to sing, dance, build, recycle, create, stimulate? Did you wanted to write? Just look at this book – pathetic! You can do it. Start writing dear reader. Did you want to be that person in that game of life? Any game? Did you ever….?

Do it. No matter how far out it feels. Just to take yourself there. That unimaginable edge of you. The new curve, the new frontier of yourself.

It's not for the weak of heart to go for it and just do, and so we who haven't found our strength yet have unrequited dreams that just sit there in the bank of the collective mind of the universe, very still or barely shuffling around. What is not used by you in this life is still likely to be created, but else where by someone else drawing on your ideas. We are feeding the collective mind with ideas all the time, all the answers to the problems of the world are already loaded up there ready to be solved! But who's going to do it? Might as well be you! Do it now or don't, but your thoughts and desires are real. Live it – that which you dream and be it for real. Trust that if a feeling or a concept came to you – you might as well be it. Become it. Embody it. Carry it through! And yes, perhaps even benefit from it on many different levels.

If you do not embody that which you dream– it can be hard to do other things later, as the material for the dream that you are crafting is ordered, yet you don't let yourself create! The material that dreams are made of is very real. It crowds, it hoards. It bunches when we keep it for a later date. Don't hoard your dreams or life becomes no easier. Only shallower breaths, smaller perspectives, higher minds but little force or creative strategy.

What about the others?

Don't count on us to listen, see or understand. Accept that success is just the process of creating, just doing – it is not receiving from the act of doing. It is the mature ability to generate not the focus of what is received through it. Don't count on us to listen, understand, even hear what you are. You must do it for you and become the process itself through which you inspire the world – that is yourself. Through this you turn and emote into greater ways of being here. Create. Do it! Clear your "Dream Pallet"! Be fresh!

To be a creator truly is to understand that creation is all it is – it may be unreciprocated, lost or forgotten, but that is not the point. The unrequited love of the creator, the poet or the writer isn't hard, it's just forgetfulness of the overall picture of us all. We do not nurture our nature sometimes, which is why we are afraid to create. That is because we forget that we are and all is…vibration.

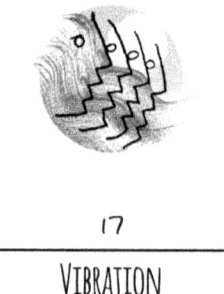

17

Vibration

That's right, we're all just vibration offcourse – the turning sea of energy that is going through it's own overall process seen and unseen. We are all just vibration and in that the encompassing feeling of truth – the oneness of us all together in one melting pot of love. We do not care if you're good or not. We don't deserve or desire you in some way and we do not expect on the soul level anything from each other. We do not care. We just experience. We are all just a turning ocean of energy. Nothing is personal here. We just vibrate.

In human truth, everything is but a little piece of the game for us, which is not bad or sad and especially not heartless. Passionless acceptance is the underlying truth of this universe despite societal values, so don't rely on us to listen, feel or understand you or your work and craft even remotely. Don't rely on us to accept you or love you more than you understand to love yourself. If you would like to be loved – love you so much that we cannot help but feel the same way too.

We aren't capable of understanding love on the most part, though we have deeply connected to the ethereal ideal of loving or caring for something out there beyond ourselves. It is impossible to love another greater than you love yourself, it truly is.

To ask a soul to vibrate to greater need to understand and hold another soul is the same as asking an atom to change it's frequency completely or to turn water into wine. It is impossible and it shouldn't be scary to realize this. We are selfish, yes, as selfish as an atom that knows it's own unique vibration more and better than any other atom because it's own self is what it is. We aren't capable of understanding or mirroring each other completely and that is beautiful. Because we are all in our own little bubbles and worlds, that is why we are so interesting to each other, that's why we are so unique. Embrace the separation between each person – it is truly marvellous.

Trust you to be you and to find what is interesting for you personally. What is true inside the very being that you are? Trust in knowing more about that. Nothing and nobody else.

The trick to the whole game of life is to just be yourself. Nobody else has the true capacity to really care or even understand you completely. You can though - only you can really understand and hold yourself. Go towards that sweet spot of inner fulfilment. Expand your auric field through going within, don't worrying about your impact on another. It's simple.

> "GO TOWARDS THAT SWEET SPOT OF INNER FULFILLMENT. EXPAND YOUR AURIC FIELD THROUGH GOING WITHIN, DON'T WORRY ABOUT YOUR IMPACT ON ANOTHER. IT'S SIMPLE."

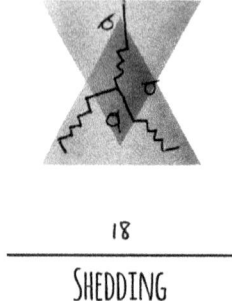

18

Shedding

Shed your presumption about who we are and how we feel about you. Nobody cares. That's right, you heard correctly. You may like to put down the book now and yes, it's consciousness would understand.

On an instinctual or natural level - nobody cares. Nobody caries another person or that person's dreams for them. Nature is self sustaining. There is no part of the natural world that is born to carry another part. It is all self efficient despite the nature of the ecosystem – we all are born to carry ourselves. To care for ourselves alone. To be ourselves for the pleasure of just being ourselves.

If you believe that carrying or caring for another is natural or even necessary as part of the natural program of this reality you would need to reconsider. "Will they be there for me?" or "Will they love me?" shouldn't be a consideration because nature figures things out for us on it's own within balanced parameters without needing someone else's backbone to support us unless we are very small young and helpless. Even then nature kicks in and the parent is enthralled in their child for the reason of it's success. We do not have to rely on one another to thrive at all, we are programmed to figure ourselves out quick and be there for us first, all else follows naturally. Nothing needed from another ever. Expectation isn't fun as it is never on track.

A person being dependant or reliable for another is a construct, which has no value in the natural world at all. We are not cogs. We are natural parts of this world.

Do not worry if we won't care and do not worry if we do care. Just be proud when you do carry you, when you carry all that is you and nothing else. No wallet maybe even with time. You need nothing, nobody to carry you unless you are a newborn. You just need you to carry - that is how you are designed, that is what nature gave you.

Shed all that isn't yours from birth and you might find that carrying yourself is very light indeed.

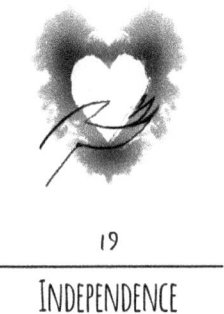

19
Independence

Independence is a birth right for everyone, it is a requirement of ANY lifetime. You have nothing but yourself. Get used to that. It is not sad, it is blissful. Every spectrum of life embodied is based entirely on the power of independence.

Go into the city alone. Go to places on your own. Alone, with nothing. See what happens! Your wallet and your phone won't cost you your life. Learn to become more independent over time. The one who walks alone dreams the biggest dreams. The spirits of the land and the people before you are there - they will support you. All is there, all is provided. It is yours – your life and the more you bloom into it with deep intensity the less likely you will want to leave.

Feelings, other people, activities that aren't for you will all seem shadow to your true life when you learn to walk alone. As you develop your independence all else sheds and exposes what you are and who you truly could become. The path is cleared and is uncluttered from all the debris of people in your life. Things become simple, streamline. You are like a supreme sports car – nothing but the basics. Easy ride into the sunset of your choosing.

Independence physically, psychically and spiritually is very hard to create as we think we need a lot more than we do. Independence in totality means no more reliance on anything. It means independence from that which you "own" – or rather that which "owns" you. Your friendships possess you. Your possessions possess you. Wallets, bags and other accessories are a keep sake for you with time when you recognise the power of you. Perhaps one day you won't even need them again, or at least understand that they are nothing without you. Just an empty piece of the modern age. You are what makes your home your home and what makes your wallet your wallet. You are.

Without your dependency nothing in your world is powerful over you. We make factors of our lives a bother with our thoughts and emotional values we place on things. Don't commit to things and people as if they were an integral part of the eco system that you live in. Earth has it's own eco system. Earth has it's own rule book. All other systems are false.

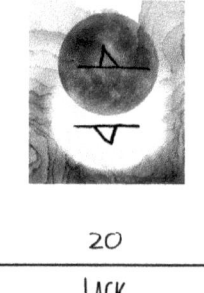

20
Lack

Lack: I have no money, I have no time, I have no body...get rid of that now. This feeling of lack is not an emptiness that you are looking at – it is the add on that you have acquired through your DNA. It is a false precept. It's not hard to alter it. Pop – it's easy to adjust your spirals by only understanding it.

If you do not feel you have something - think again or consider yourself greedy.

Do you need that presence of something else in your life? Do you even need that scented candle, dog, home, person? Yes? They are an aid? No? Good. Let them loose. If you recognise that you don't need an aid in anything or anyone you possess or want to attain - loss is lost. If you know you need no aids in what you are – you are good. You're free of the most damaging DNA mutation. Lack.

If you recognise and release all that you grasp for, you would perhaps understand that all is already gotten - that you are already complete. You are true, you are for you, you get you - nothing else can be gotten if you get yourself. No training wheels needed for this magic bike!

You get me? You get yourself.

If all feels gotten, all loss is forgotten.

Get rid of your need for more. It won't give you any rest otherwise.

Go! It's time to move on.

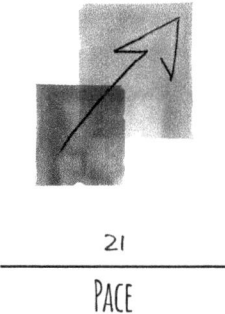

21
PACE

There is always at least one thing to move right away from and into the new dimension. Dimensional shifting is constant and ia always an option.

Each thought and feeling has a tendency to take us into a new dimension if we so desire. Each smile and yoga posture can navigate us to the next breath that opens the new doors. The shift is very possible and is always open, so move towards that which is brighter, lighter and more intense for you always.

Flow with your senses!

There are bigger shifts too, or what we call land marks: that job, that person, that place etc. Move on and start walking now. Each step and breath opens you up to greater possibility, a greater image of yourself, a greater stability, a greater sense.

You don't need a thing from this world that you think you do so don't worry where you do and do not belong. If you can't get up and get moving by yourself, you'll never quite make it. Why not make it? Go, shift in the direction of your choosing. You can indeed do it right this minute.

You will never make your life what it is about if you don't just up and go. Make yourself fresh, become greater, enjoy. There is no story that benefits from stagnation.

> "DIMENSIONAL SHIFT IS CONSTANT AND IS ALWAYS AN OPTION."

22
SELFISHNESS

Being yourself – that is what being you is about. (Revisit the first couple of chapters if you are still concerned about you as a being).

If you are not you –then who are "you"? – just a label? A label wasting time. Don't waste yourself on a career or a job or a placement…ever! Start walking. Start moving, behave as you and be what you are. Just as you are, just as you be. Just like that.

Are you selfless when you are staying behind for others or becoming something other than your complete being? No. Move on. That is a false program.

Selfish people aren't bad. They are just far enough in themselves enough to know better. We are conditioned to be afraid of it because we have built many societies based on selflessness as virtue and so nobody is embodied, everything becomes a system very quickly.

Move on from the need to be self-less, as that deems you unsteady in yourself. Giving and nurturing of others should be as a sort of surprise - a funny momentum that has no push. It just generates, just happens for no reason. To struggle at becoming selfless is a crime. It is a false way towards momentum and yes, nobody wins. Only takes and gives, drains and disfigures, creating problems anew again and again. Cycles are created through "positive action" without the right momentum that cannot be of much use. So, unless it is powerfully obvious and easy – do not commit to selfless tasks. Just become instead. Learn about yourself and the world a little bit more.

Selfishness is no sin. It is a healthy part of your system.

Become more self-ish. Understand that selfish things and understandings of others are normal, natural as you are designed especially to be at your own centre, nobody else's. No specific God or Deity is something to circulate around for that reason. Only draw from which you have inside already for that reason. And yes. Inside is where God lives too! Show yourself the dimension of your true gifts through yourself and through the exploration of what you need and feel you deserve. Explore that.

My needs are....

They will tell so much about you! Why not listen to them?

It is true that selfishness in it's extremes is ugly or beastly – but only because it is hard to work with self when it has been forgotten and misplaced for such a long time. The needs that haven't been met for a long time stagnate and become overbearing creating all sorts of up-turnings in oneself. Don't be afraid of your selfish needs. After they are understood and cleared, this new selfish fire is just you knowing you better, and no one else. The needs and wants will not pursue when understood.

So why not stop reading, dream out loud, see what that brings instead! Be selfish now. However,

If you cannot fathom that being selfish or self-bound is good, please go on reading, there is more to learn maybe. If you can understand that it all just comes down to YOU - start doing! Forget all books and programs.

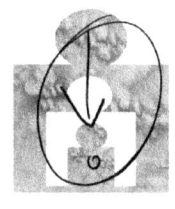

23

START

Start right here as you are. That's right, right here is good.

You can't understand what you need to do? Are you scattered at the prospect of a new beginning? In that case, who you are becoming better start running! If you really can't understand what you need to do in your life – if you're following steps that seem unclear - start jogging, start playing, start right here.

This is your body, there is no other priority. If nurtured and honoured, the body can show you where to start without need to think or feel. It will just happen. The way becomes clear through inner activation.

If you have mastered jogging and you still sit here reading – ok, good, you're on the go! Start carrying you without anything else that you don't need. No car, no wallet. Believe in what you've got! Believe in what you are born with! if you cannot do that, if you feel stuck and meaningful somehow – time to release. Start embarrassing yourself a bit!

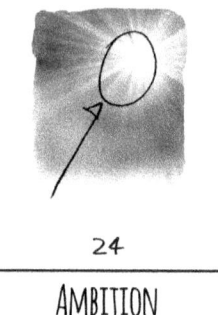

24
AMBITION

Ambition isn't a bright and shiny thing that we'd like to imagine or believe it to be. It's not God given, it's not powerful, neither is it beautiful. We were created simple. Ambition is the evolutionary add on. There is plenty of shadow there in that little glitch in the system. Ego. It's a tricky player in the DNA game.

Here ego is good. Ego makes ambition take hold and so you evolve through it and maybe even take many others with you! If there is deep need for evolution within then yes, ambition is the necessary player in the game of life for now. Paired with ego they make a special shadow team that makes it all happen in ways, but then what?

Then there has to be lulls and plateaus to let other forces play the game.

If we cannot feel ourselves naturally just as we are, if we cannot walk and enjoy, if we do not breathe and experience enlightenment – we get possessed by the need to succeed at something else and through that we design a new adventure or a new tribulation or both. Just to overcome something. So, take ambition as an aid to greater consciousness, but in that isn't anything natural or freeing. Just more rubix cubes to solve with eventual death of ego.

Ego grows, you grow. As light grows - the void grows too. In the way of quantum understanding, you are more void than matter or, if you'd like to imagine - your light is not as vast as your void, so understand that - you are a dark being and that is natural. It's good!

So what do you want to do? What do you want to accomplish? Void is a great accomplice to those who are looking to succeed in the end offering only peace anyway. Just light.

If you cannot just be, if you are struck by the need to "succeed" - stop thinking you as an angel and start acting. The more you sit back and behave as something else while you want to be somewhere else, the larger your ego grows underneath and perhaps the larger you get (physically) - but the dream stays the same. Motionless. Use your ego and the unrest within to succeed! Just to show yourself the way forward…into what you could have been anyway – just at peace.

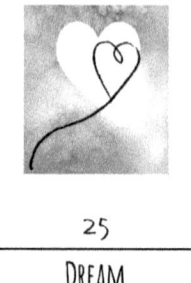

25
DREAM

Be the dream. That's not a problem, right? How hard is it to see though…that you are already the dream? There is no need to truly be or embody any other "self" but the current state. You are the perfect dream of God right now exactly as you are.

Well, what is this dream thing anyway? Look around where you are – THAT is it – that is you. Each detail, sound and smell. It is all you and who you have come to be in the connective future past and present – through all space and time. That's right. This moment right now literally exactly as it is – is you. This is all you need to knit your new reality from. Just watch how you concentrate on that which you see. In the way you accent and perceive is the moulding of your new world, your next dream and new reality. So watch for that. How you perceive what is around is creating your new world as you sit here right now.

How do you feel about it all so far? That is the answer to your dreams.

The cars you don't want to drive anymore maybe. Cities you don't want to live in anymore maybe. The smog, the traffic, the prices. Maybe money you don't want to play with anymore. Hmm. There's a lot you don't want anymore in this whirl of a dream that you're connected to. This book maybe and the trees or the writer that suffered for it. President Bush, Trump, whoever is the new face of the mechanical structure on top of this planet. This dream that touches you – where you sleep eat and live. Is it a dream in which there are aspects that hurt and annoy? Well,

You are the dream, so you yourself are the element that unbinds you from greater creation.

If you do not like it – that dream that you're part of – that's because you haven't mastered "you" yet. If you are still complaining about the world today in a large general scale or small detail - bad luck as you are dissatisfying your journey further. All is one, so your perceptions bring back to you what it is that you do not like about your world like waves bring debris to a beach.

Please stop complaining and relate to all things with love! If you cannot – you must walk to find that which you do enjoy. For some walking from one situation right into the next situation is difficult just yet. Means it's time to relate, to be in some thought.

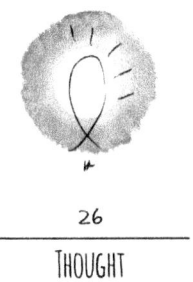

26
Thought

If you're not sure in who you are here in this dream yet, start thinking. That is, think here before you are able to master non-thinking and trust. When in non thought - nature carries you naturally and effortlessly along the currants of the divine dream. The greater dream.

Thought is not created. It is programmed. That is hard to know or understand as we do attach ourselves to our thoughts and so we suffer. Continue thinking before you can understand that thinking original thoughts is almost impossible. We're all in a collective melting pot that has been stirring itself for eons, so let go of all thought as you let them wash over you in peace. Thought is ego, void. It isn't as important as we are told, it is not becoming or embodying anything, not even your brain…thought is merely just reminiscing, simple processing. Nothing more. And it is the processing of another life's events from long ago usually passed on through the grape vine of souls. It isn't even yours. Let it go.

Thought and constant processing is a life of a computer. 1 and 0, black and white - it is backwards and it's not servicing the greater experience of your life unless you truly are stuck and you need to think to return to the common grooves of the world. When sparingly used, thought becomes a world of mastery. Reliance on thought makes ripples on your reality spectrum where thoughts indeed can bring you magic, yes, but in time those ripples create insufficiency in other ways if forced or stressed. In forceful thought the fabric of reality is pulled and you my friend become something else that you may not like to be, as thought without poise does create disseat. Overthinking links to trouble and old stories that are best left alone. It creates cycles and psychic depths that you do not benefit from treading. Try to think less and just trust life already!

The best of the best aren't deep thinking people. They are just open arms and hearts. They pitch into the caldron of collective thought only fishing out what is ripe and best for the time being thanks to poise of thought. It is not the process of genius that is overthought and overdone. It is the process of labour and labour seldom creates results that are worthy of the work. True genius comes from sincerity of the heart that is tuned into itself. The thoughts only follow the heart when needed. They are a minor part in the process of your unfolding.

If you are intellectually advanced or very brain orientated person that is fine. That is very well understood in today's comical trends. There is lots of work to do for you though, that's all. If for now thought is your magic – make it yours. Maybe then when you process enough and get tired of other people's information cycles through past present and future and in time you will shut out the cycles of thought. You'll still once and for all. You'll start walking and experiencing finally – a miracle is possible then, as by walking you're walking out of the who you identify with eventually and into that best described as Eden, or heaven.

This book here is not a collection of thoughts that were forged by my brain. There was no thought process involved in this book at all. It was given to me through the collective mind…by people who thought too much…and so here it is. Your thoughts perhaps on a plate – merely collected by a thoughtless mind and an open soul.

27
Thoughtlessness

Absolutely no thought.

Peace is possible and lots easier than imagined. We just have to stop glamorizing thought and the need to be in "control" that's all.

You know this feeling very well perhaps - the feeling when you just pick up that sandwich as you're hungry or when you talk to somebody because they feel good. Words come out lazy and not strung together. Perhaps you don't know what you'll utter before you do. That is thoughtless conversation and it isn't bad – it is honest! It is at peace, at home with itself. Words and actions just are. You are endless or become understood anyway. When you do not process, you are not controlled. Your heart matches your action and in that is your charisma. All connects, all is not distorted or turbulent, all simplifies, all becomes love.

No thought - just impulse of the universe made real through you.

Just be here. Savour this. It is a nice feeling – it is not loss and it is not idle mindedness.

If you are thoughtless you are close to peace. Just be here if you are here. Don't worry. If you think it is dangerous or unhuman not to think - you have lots of business to do here and sort your self identity out in the process of it. There is courage needed then if you were taught that something within you was so bad you had to be careful of who you are if you aren't possessed by thought.

If you are in fear and you think you have got danger if you don't think - you're indoctrinated - time to jest at your life!

28
HUMOUR

Jest! Laugh about it all. All is genius and yes, in some funny unique way, all life is humorous. You're nothing, we are nothing, yet it's all possible and it is all created! We are all mostly just space floating around the great ocean of light, or is it light that is floating around the great ocean of depth? It's a funny little world we live in. I do not know.

All you have gained, all you have done means almost nothing and the more you parade it the more you parade the illusion of yourself around where you go. What happens in seriousness? You mould to the lie you have become and it won't let you go until you see the joke beneath. Don't worry about what you haven't or have done. Don't worry. It's all an aid in you becoming more yourself, more peaceful, more loving, more loyal. Nothing else. The ending is only the beginning always, so laugh about it immortal!

Humour is the burst of light as there are no boundaries where there once were. It is the joke of God, and the laughter of God too.

If you do not want to be here yourself wherever you are, however you look to yourself, that is fine. You can hide behind your trendy palace or your sexy vehicle, your social standing, spouse or friends, even religion. Whatever you do - it's ok. If you're hiding – you're just lost and we know it within us beyond pity. We know you aren't coming to dance the dance of life.

The joke of your life is still a success. Even though you might not realise it all the time. But, after this life, we all make jest eventually of our previous selves so much that we go ahead and do it all again!

How to feel no longer sad? What is the opposite of sadness? Dance and humour! Can you find it? Why is it important anyway?

If you want to start a new cycle of creation the best way to start is to laugh or to smile at the previous cycle with ease. This signifies completion. Can you find laughter in any way? No? Bad idea to start something fresh. Push the joke inwards where it hurts maybe. If it stills for too long it can't be found sometimes, but sometimes being very sad or angry creates more humour and light later! Can you laugh at something? This little conversation we are having perhaps? Good. You're moving onwards!

Don't be afraid to be loud about your humour! It's imperative that we become more open to do so!

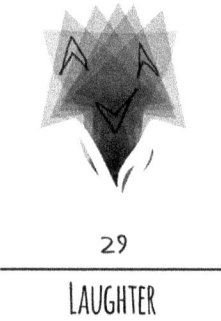

29

Laughter

A laugh is all you need! It is the only thing that can burst through all barriers sometimes.

You don't need a thing if you have a laugh. You don't have a thing if you can't!

If you can't laugh at your family or your car or your job or your placement in society, you aren't living. If you are still struggling though you're on your 3rd marriage and 2nd set of kids, well, you're lost my friend. Lost.

Start laughing now. Is there something that you do over and over? Is there a pattern that you create with people? Is there a pattern of security or is there a job related pattern maybe? Do you work too hard or too little? Is there a different person that you become sometimes? Laugh at that now. Take the chance to burst through all your fear of yourself – become buoyant with light!

In the darkest moments – laughter will catch you. No wonder many stand up comedians pitch so much of their materials out of shadows. Shadow and light – they are one. In depth, laughter will push you through. Without laughter in great depths, there is no light.

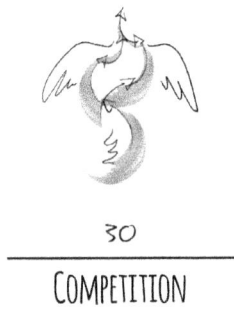

30
Competition

Compete only with yourself. Nothing and nobody else.

If you can't create intention with no competition between people in the mix, if you are still looking to other people's values in comparison to your own experience - we have a problem. If your competitive nature is the only edge that powers you through - we've got to find another way out here. The competitive edge that's so wonderfully paraded in the West is a great big shadow that sucks in like nobody's business! Before you know it many things and parts of you are lost and misplaced. It's not a good idea to mould to competition with others, but it isn't bad to compete against yourself only.

Have you got to get things done? Do it for you. Do you want to get that body? Do it for you. You've got to get that partner? Don't pretend it's for the "two of you". It's for You! It's no good if it's for mum or dad, but yes, trust it if it's just for you. Play with your own desire

and see how fun the game gets. If there is a creative justice or a great light born out of self competing – then yes, it is in order. You are the worthiest and the most exhilarating opponent for yourself. Through self competition talent is created into something phenomenal. Genius minds are born here. But don't do it for anyone else. Make it yours.

"IN THE DARKEST MOMENTS —
LAUGHTER WILL CATCH YOU."

31

Negativity

Are you trying too hard to see faults here? Is it a cycle perhaps?

Are you being at fault by seeing the fault as an obstruction or dent? Don't worry, each fault you see without need is quite often yours to keep or yours to start with on the moment of it's "creation" in your mind! If you like to pick at people, yourself or anything that happens to catch your senses badly or your self image poorly, welcome.

Welcome to hell.

Things can get very easily spiralled and expressed here that do not suit the individual later. Things get messy fast and though it was a harmless pattern at first maybe to look for perfection and yet be so aroused by the negative components of life - these negative components turn around and they do ingrain, which makes it hard to move with time. If you are finding yourself ingrained into your own negativity and nit picking process – it is good to step off and admit that you are a negative person to yourself. Admit your judgements and distaste for things. Begin to see it as a dark joke about yourself and perhaps underneath it all – there is just a small child who never got to play.

If you can't have things to you liking and you have to keep on trying to make things brighter or better all the time you're in hell, enjoy that feeling. Understand it or at least try not to do any more negative thinking here.

Perhaps through chaos and confusion you will be able to shed your need for specification of your world – the need for having things "just so". In many ways perfectionism and mental disorders are clearly linked. Fixation makes it so, even on small levels. The inability to be in creation and the serendipity of it all moulds individuals who are stuck up or in ways unable to just move on from what they do not like, creating stuck feelings and stuck creations. Much of the sex drive or the divine sexual force is spent on that which isn't working and so energy wanes from the body much too quickly with age. It would be nice to enjoy without inner argument, wouldn't it? What is that cure for a perfectionist's mind? Chaos.

32

CHAOS

Chaos isn't angry, chaos isn't dangerous. Chaos is the natural thing that happens when things get a little bit too mild and subdued with unjust foundations underneath. War happens, distortion takes place. Chaos is the answer to a life underneath which there isn't much substance or depth.

There are likely many things that you aren't rebelling against maybe. Many of us have great barriers out of deep need to keep things tidy in the past. We have all perhaps been pushed into a mould somehow in our lives as teenagers or children, being able to do things in only certain formulas. If that is you – mess it up! Mess up your predictable experiences! Don't hold on to any system for a while just to let your own light be louder and more powerful than the constraints that have been created for you! Mess up your bed, your hair, your relationship, all your systems!

Mess up! If you can't perceive an unhappy client or your life being out of place or your partner being in line with something slightly different to your idea of "good" - mess it up. Throw things out or at least complain in public where other people are aggravated by you and your need to have things "just so". Be public about your constraints! Be ridiculous! Mess up your perfectly created sense of self!

Mess is good. Most people with great talent and achievement have created great messes at least from something in their life. In chaos there is formula free opportunity for creativity. A blast waiting to happen. A quantum shift.

Mess up or get up! If you can't control or shake what is upsetting, get up and walk away from it. Rebel at that which is holding you stiff and agitated, unhappy yet needing to get things right. Walk away if you can't yet shake and shiver things out of your system. If you cannot walk away – you must think again and start seeing the truth of you – the real you – however untameable that must feel. Learn to breathe that fire, dragon!

What is going on? Perhaps you are getting things wrong? Is something wrong? Good. It's a chance at a greater life!

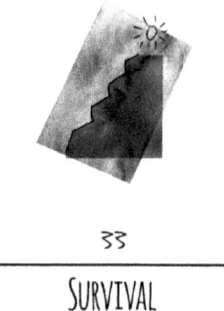

33

SURVIVAL

Survival. "Making a living" is not right for anybody. It's for no-body.

If you aren't breathing, feeling and explaining what life is to yourself through motion and deep inertia, you aren't alive you know. So what kind of living can be made here? Limited.

If you are just coping - you are sitting at that desk job or you are playing games with your self, well, you're wrong there. You are very wrong, and though you might think that one day it'll bring success, it won't give you back those years lost or those precious cells that won't be able to regenerate fast if you don't exercise them and trust them to reform the way they should through pure inertia and the success of Everyday Enjoyment!

Life is for the living, not for making a living. Let your body live and breathe fully. If you can't continue to feel alive, what you are creating is a sort of grey existence that can barely support what is not supported by nature. Nature doesn't support interdependency or inability to experience what your body wants you to! When walking around in undesirable circles, your life becomes unresolved and you rely on the false system of monetary rebalancing indeed a lot more than on the body – as it doesn't want to trust after long cycles of self abuse. All unnatural cycles won't last and your body will suffer.

Take your time with life. It's ok if you don't know what you are doing or why you are doing it for. It is best to stop and relate then to keep on going in the wrong direction.

Life is supportive, God will support you, we are always listening. Just trust in that. If you do not trust and you are concentrating on making ends meet people can't reach out, things won't happen, nothing can free in a world of strong belief. Yes – the monetary system is the new belief system it seems.

Concentrate on your energy and how much of it you are filtering through your being. Concentrate on your evolution. The rest isn't a thing to concentrate on. It's just a mere offshoot of your life, not the main parameter of it.

Be still if you can. If you can't perhaps there's more to address further.

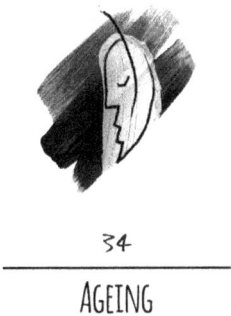

34
Ageing

Feeling tired yet unable to sit still and be? Ageing is here. It gives you more and yet it will not give you a thing.

Ageing happens globally lately (for last few thousand years) for the wrong reasons, mostly because of the mess we are in as a global society of beings on this land (apart from some very marginal cultures). Is ageing a product of cause and effect? No. It is not. It is a product of wasteful thinking, dreaming and needing, the product of unused feeling and uncredited inertia. Unsaid words. Unloved moments. Unattainable dreams. It's not a product of us as a species, ageing is what happens when the inner voice isn't declared. Humans age rapidly when the inner voice isn't heard, when instead we choose to commit the mistake of "making do". As we just make do - we make youth disappear.

Is ageing what we need to know, fight or reduce? No - at least let's understand the thing and get on with it….

Ageing happens to anyone who is not able to be and feel alive.

> "AGEING IS WHAT HAPPENS WHEN THE INNER VOICE ISN'T DECLARED."

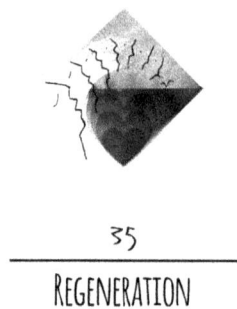

35
Regeneration

Regeneration.

Reproduction is not just about creating more of yourself "else where" through another being…. reproduction is in fact within you and it is constant. All is full and empty, contracting and expanding, being born and dying, all is constantly glowing and recreating more of itself. You reproduce yourself anew top to bottom every seven years according to science. You are a self reproducing creature and that is a fact. Celebrate it! Anything is possible!

Yes, you might have a child or three, that is great but if you can't reproduce yourself fast you're not reproducing correctly. Your main point of being here is to self replicate further and that's nothing to do with child birth. Yes, our ancestors got it a bit wrong there: hello overpopulation, goodbye free will and optimum opportunity.

Your own regeneration is to do with your own emotional, physical and spiritual research that connects to you a brand new possibility for LIFE as You! A bigger better and prouder version of you in the same body made possible through your work on your inner worlds. Regeneration takes place naturally when you believe in yourself and alchemise all that you experience thoroughly.

If you can, start walking, start breathing and yes, start doing - that will give you more stamina and a deeper expanding need to be here! In that is your youthful glow and evolving body. You live within a form that automatically is able to receive all the latest trends in frequency that translate to a greater self generating, faster renewing physical makeup every single day. Your regeneration is within. Always available, always in the swing!

What you see in your world through attainment is only the tip of the iceberg. The way that you live your life and believe what you believe is only part of the evolutionary work you are creating here as a soul. In your own body, your own creative flow, you are creating leaps for us all as you learn to integrate yourself into greater efficiency and communion through mastering of your own energy. You help us all know so much more through your own physical and spiritual expansion that you later share with us through deep communion within yourself as you rest though you may not understand it yet.

When you are at peace and you go within – you go up into the collective consciousness grids simultaneously, where you can give us that which we are looking for and exchange ideas, downloads and information as you like. Therefor your sleeping patterns and meditation patterns connect you to your greater being more than any other form of existence. We all do this in our sleep and waking life always. Nobody is missed out in the collective mind. This is not conscious for most people but we are all hooked up and extremely connected. We would love to know more about you if you are a self regenerating individual as that is where we are all going to be soon!

Stop procrastinating or yawning already - just do it! The more you achieve regeneration or rewiring of your previous self, the greater creator you become! How fun! Create, compete with you and start fresh!

If you are tired my friend, you are out of luck. If you are still here, receiving very little stimulus or inspiration, yet still reading - you have a little or a big problem here (depending on the opportunity for growth you are providing yourself).

> "REGENERATION TAKES PLACE NATURALLY WHEN YOU BELIEVE IN YOURSELF AND ALCHEMISE ALL THAT YOU EXPERIENCE THOROUGHLY."

36
Fatigue

Tired means "nobody". Tired means opted out and left the building…even if it is just for a few minutes. Tired feelings aren't welcome in the collective scheme unless the tired is used as a bland frequency to bounce energy against. The tired are welcomed only as an opportunity for someone else, not as an equal part of the game. Tiredness creates great problems without and within for all of us. That is because we do not know how to handle it yet.

If you are here, yet you aren't here, it's important to recognise this. If you are not fully looking, evolving and loving being here, you need to step up and you need to do it fast. Even if it is told to you that you can't or you shouldn't. If you can't be that person you are embodying at all, if you can't even handle the energetic strain of being yourself right now - you have a lot of self motivating to do!

Sometimes tired is just the way of the world it seems. It is the family-created dependency cycles and deep need for "nurture" – it is fine to recognise this as part of your family, as this dependency and need to be small or shameful has created itself into a global disease – fatigue of the wealthy, fatigue of the poor, fatigue of the needy, fatigue of the tired of experience people.

Even though fatigue is a part of a pattern - there is need to motivate through it, to burn through it with your strength. Perhaps we don't have to concentrate so much on pure survival now, but the motivation has to be found, and perhaps it might be this:

Creation of closure with something. Completion of something so you can then bounce back onto your feet once more!

Completion is an easy task. Do something you can complete and marvel at it. Spike up your interest in yourself by what is doable and enjoyable. Be it and become more important through the glory of completion for now if being you just isn't cutting it yet. If you can – show it! Show that you've done something and perhaps we will smile at it too.

Try to make room to shake, create and succeed or indeed fail, as in failure is humour and in humour there's rapture of a new world to come! Strive forward! Make the fool that you are out of what you thought wasn't foolish before, start living fresh!

If you do not want to be tired but you are, you're even more a mess as you do not understand the cause of it, so let's have a look at some possible energetic causes of fatigue in the next sequence of thoughts...

No need to look too far out or too far back. Let's look at you now. Trouble isn't something on the outside. It is something within.

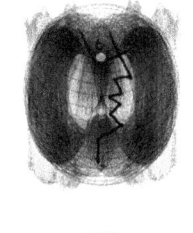

37

Trouble

Are you standing straight? No? Fix that. Are you walking in line? No? Fix that. Are you having to breathe deep sometimes as you don't usually breathe enough? What is your diet choice? Are you hungry? And the list goes on. There is always something to fix right now and that something small may change your life forever :D

Fix those things before you can fix everything else. Anything "out there" has a little answer right here - within yourself. Your body is your fortress; it is the beautiful vessel for your soul. It matters more than any other thing you have on your list of things to do! So, before you start worrying about what could or should be wrong here, start seeing the obvious – how you carry yourself, what is it that you feel, what are the physical symptoms of your life.

For a healthy glowing person there shouldn't be any aches pains or dislocations. There should be a feeling of being fine – a fine feeling – it is when you are feeling very little in the body but a flame of life is strong. A passion, a force. Something deep and nurturing within.

If you aren't glowing yet and you want to be – find it and fix it. Something about you right now is ready to fall into place with a little tender love and care. It always is! If you can't physically cope with having your human form – there has to be some serious devotion poured all over it. If you have lost touch with yourself, there has to be much connection and association with your body again in order to allow it to build trust again. Bodies can do that – the organs and cells can indeed disassociate from us if we haven't been feeling well about them, if we haven't been looking after them with love and care, if we haven't been listening. If you cannot be with pride and love embodied as that which you are born to be, that is the first thing that must be addressed before any other problems are addressed at all.

Before you trouble shoot any part of your life be yourself first. Be it – the person you have been designed by nature to be. Centre here. On you! Then - decide later what you want to create in this life as the human you are – the real you. If your troubles are here for the fact that you can't yet breathe properly, sit straight, be still or stand tall, you're in luck, as this book is an attempt to kick your butt into the new frontier of being!

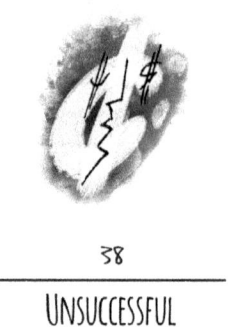

38

Unsuccessful

Are you tired? You're broke?

Are you struggling with something that is not for you? Are you not able to generate enough income for the expensive things you have decided you might need? You aren't broke. You're just stupid. Nothing to see here! If you recognise this, please give up on what you think it is you might need and see the full picture please.

If you however do not get it yet, please read on

If you're not stupid, just broke, the lesson is easy. Fix yourself. Fix your face with a smile and a powerful yell. Fix your body with an exercise or a pathway to walk on. Fix your walk and your inner talk with creative ways to be on this Earth. Fix yourself.

If you can't fix yourself, you truly are broke. Energetically broke. Time to see a specialist (see my details on the last page) or read on and help yourself.

39
Independence

You don't need anything you've got already let alone something more! That's a simple human truth. You do not need even this book telling you how to live your life. You are born free! Does that frighten you?

If you think you need something still - you're scared of yourself. Maybe it's time to start feeling what that fear might be and what it's reason is. Through understanding your fear of yourself you can find your freedom and start living to the full. If you aren't able to just be yourself - you have fear of it. So stop that, start feeling!

See all the bits: the bossy bits, the strong bits, the enigmatic bits – all the bits of you as divine. Start seeing the whole picture of yourself without sacrifice of any part of you.

In feeling through your energy without censorship there is great freedom!

"YOU ARE BORN FREE. DOES THAT FRIGHTEN YOU?"

40
Fearfulness

With fear, you have to be patient. You have to be. If you do not like it and you do not want to look at it - you ignore it or make it a normal part of your daily life - you are my friend are in deep struggle. Pain, headaches, all of that – just symptoms of fear. Our society runs on fear as fuel! We do not need it anymore yet we still include it like a spicy sauce over a dish of life. We need to stop creating need for it, we need to stop saying "it's ok" or glamourize it as something sweet and innocent. There is no preciousness in fear – only losses.

Ailments of any kind: big or small is trapped fear inside, so what to do about it?

Firstly, you might have to recognise that you are in fear. Secondly you might have to stop identifying your fear as part of your identity or a part of good behaviour. Then – Laugh!

Unsure about laughter? Return to thought number 29 on laughter just in case and read it some more

Do you know what else combats all inner fear? Sound! Sound breaks through all fear and mindlessness.

"It is all singing a song to you."

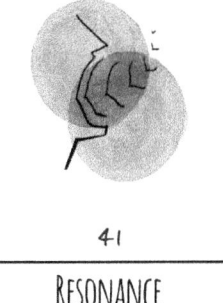

41
Resonance

Voice is sound and sound is healing. We are blessed with it from birth! Sound is creative ability, matter is sound. Sound is God. It is the former of worlds. It is the closest thing to a miracle today. And it is here always available to you through your voice and other instruments!

How to find your hidden fears? The sound of your voice a tell tale sign of your inner worlds. Test it every day.

If you cannot emit sound with pride and your voice doesn't ring, you have hidden fear. If you cannot listen to another person's voice or song, there is creation overhaul inside that doesn't want to surrender. Listen, understand sound. Pleasure in sound. Feel it, it is you talking to you whatever you are listening to right now. All noise that you hear is resonance made for you somehow, so admit yourself to the sound of your life as it is right now:

The tap, the traffic outside, the birds, the trees – it is all singing the song of you.

If you cannot express or sing out loud with all beauty of your voice, if you can't punch through the silence or through the awkward moment with fearless joy - there is a block. You have to freely produce sound. You have to create. You are human.

Sound generates matter: this Earth, you, the pyramids and all sorts of great things. You are actually vibration that is just sound in light form. Be aware of the vibration that is you. Start sounding out loud and be proud about it!

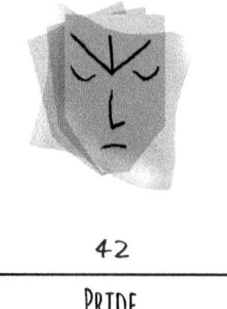

42
Pride

What is pride in this world anyway?

If you are not proud of you just being you – you might have a problem to deal with. Straighten up, straighten out. If you have no deep thoughts or understanding of being you and if you have no true need of being you - then sit down start thinking straight. If you can't understand how you can think yourself proud – perhaps it's time to find a helper or healer to aid you there. Natural pride is phenomenon that is not usually seen these days but it should be inherited through your family line. If it isn't or if it's been taken away from you by your upbringing – there needs to be considerate work. You might need a great upheaval or big push to gather enough self esteem again!

If you only gain pride through respect you achieve on your own or through other people, that's not good either. There is no need for conditions. You are enough.

In many ways, pride is just Self Love.

You don't need to do a thing. Just be proud. Be it. Now.

"YOU HAVE SUCCEEDED A LOT ALREADY! YOU GREW UP – A LOT – IN JUST ONE LIFETIME!"

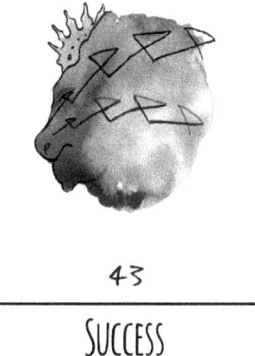

43

Success

You have succeeded already! You grew up - a lot - in just one lifetime!

Yeah you got tall or not too tall but in any case much taller than an egg cell in your mama's belly that's for sure. Success is independent of it's polarity – if you are and you are evolving always – you are successful!

Just to grow out of an egg into a person that is able to then grow up independent of a womb – it is a feat of nature! It is the very basis of success!

You got the option to be born. You got the voice and you got the physique that can scream, yell, make babies, produce information, manifest and play with all sorts of things! You are free and yes you are human! Just think of all the wonderful things you are already a success at and all the wonderful things you are able to succeed in still!

So, now what?

Well, you better not regret being here. Regret for growing is a bad thing! You grew up as a side effect of choice after choice after choice that….

God made for you.

It's not just you. It's everything that was made for you in order to exist and be – it is the gift of being here and a success of life that you must cherish.

"…AS A SIDE EFFECT OF CHOICE AFTER CHOICE THAT GOD MADE FOR YOU."

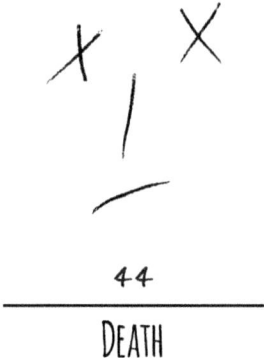

44
Death

Fun fact. God can kill you any time.

Yes, you can go any time.

You can be on an aeroplane flying off to a beautiful place and get lost in the ocean. Life is a surprising thing and can end abruptly. All things can heal, all can break, all can happen, but God is marvelling at you and there for - you live. You are not able to be if you aren't seen and adored by God… the all or yes, the being that is all things. You are watched and always felt by all that is and offcourse you are connected to a greater scheme. When you no longer fit your mould you are placed in a different energy field where you can attract a different type of solution and death is one of those solutions, but offcourse through prayer and the Need To Live – you are back in the game.

The all is able to betray your existence at any point, to connect you to a new one, but it hasn't. Because you are loved. If you are here alive and kicking, you best be in celebration as the world is celebrating you, hence you exist. You are still a precious part of this amazing well thought out and developed matrix. Nobody cares specifically, that is true, but yet, it's here. All is waiting to meet you deeper and deeper. You are here – you are not forgotten and yes, you need to be here for many of us are indeed in love with what you hold. We are in awe of you in some way if you are in existence and. We would like to see you develop as you are.

We want to know your story.

We are all listening to you constantly as you tell it.

So if you are still here, know you are wanted and loved. You are here and you are welcome. Enjoy it!

45
Enjoyment

Yeah, that is right. Just…enjoyment? That is all that this life is truly about.

Enjoyment - it has to be special, it has to be yours. Not what they have on TV as the perfect "couple" moment. Not what they have on the billboard as the "perfect gang" moment. Not what they have in the infomercials as the "family picnic", no….your special moment crafted out of the special way in which you specifically enjoy the moment. Perhaps it is with another, perhaps it is further inwards within you – the moment of enjoyment is completely different for everyone as each moment is also completely unique in itself.

Your moment. There is a special energy of it for you, different from anyone else's, and it has to be just for you alone.

Yes. It might be a secret moment of joy. It might be an explosive one, but the great news is – in many ways you are absolutely unlimited in these special moments. Absolutely unlimited.

Further inwards are the greatest joys.

> "WE WANT TO KNOW YOUR STORY.
> WE ARE ALL LISTENING TO YOU CONSTANTLY AS YOU TELL IT."

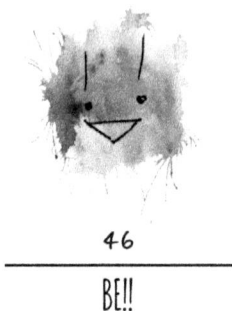

46
BE!!

That's right you are here and you have this great chance now.

Stop what you are doing and what you are wishing and thinking. It's a good chance to smell the roses and really feel that nothing is to do here anymore. Take this very special window right as you are - as an opportunity that supplies you with the most gracious pause to end a sequence and start another- to be still and empty, completely unbound by all things is to be. Just be.

Be taken back to you beyond space and time, be taken back again to the eternal now. Something is well done. You have time now. Take a breather….are you still reading? Stop. Feel this moment. It is enjoyment…feel and release! Be.

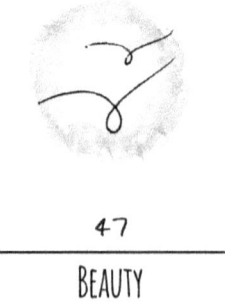

47
BEAUTY

You're in heaven.

You can be there any time no matter where or with whom on the planet you are! it's just a matter of dimensions that are navigated simply by a shifting in consciousness! You don't have to read a book or have something in front of you as a sort of symbol of it. There is no true place for you to be to find it. There is no boundary. Heaven is here if we just release the previous consciousness state. Becoming you - simply enjoyment of your moment that you are having - that is heaven indeed.

You don't need to become anything to shift dimensions, they are here already – no training necessary! Just feel what you do, the quality of it all – which then becomes the primary mechanism for the consciousness shift. As you explore the nuance between things and the sensory connectivity of all things to you – the feeling of love is overwhelming. Closer to heaven just means deeper into the light of you. The love of you. The joy of it. It is all inside, and yes, forever has been.

If you want to, you can reach out and come into this dimension….if you want to. And that's the curse there. Because you have to want it – heaven that is unconditional. Without wanting or accepting it as a possibility - you can't be there. So how to be there then? Be still…feel watch and listen…shhhh

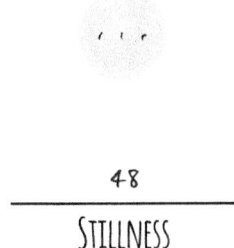

48
STILLNESS

Sometimes when you are still - be totally still then.

Not half way on the toilet with your cell phone still. Be really still and not say a word or think a thing.

It's as if you are in an elevator going towards something or away from something when you are still; in stillness dimensions change though you do not notice it. It is sweet yet cunning this way. Within this is readiness – to change, to flower. To go another way.

Ready to wake up into a new dimension? Savasana if you will…

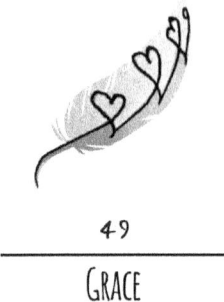

49
GRACE

The grace of God. There is no good God, bad God. No Devil or Creator. We are "it" - just here exploring ourselves. Surprise! Namaste, yes the God spark in me is in understanding of the God spark in you indeed! All is very much insane to the human mind.

There is "a" God though and it is in the collective mind of all beings – just the one frequency that interlinks everyone. It is one and was never separate or in any way incomplete.

If you are afraid of it as a separate component of your reality - you are obviously not together inside. As you depart from God and the being of all creation – you become lost without cause.

Surrender to one God in all things and the truth becomes obvious. The energy that you are here embodying is real. It is loved, cared for, seen, supported, marvelled at and is in many ways (beyond our inner most understanding) – is entirely deeply and carefully understood. You are constantly held and supported. Always.

If you cannot seed the feelings of being held with others (lots of them) as part of the same cloth of the Now, well, you're in the wrong - here is why:

"YOU ARE CONSTANTLY HELD AND SUPPORTED ALWAYS."

50
Solitude

Solitude - a dip into the ocean of oneness – it is clear single mindedness that cannot prevent you from trying to find ways into other people's dreams, but it does concentrate you within so deeply that you can grow and evolve better into new cycles - unharmed by your own decision process based on the collective melting pot of the beings that surround you. A clear taste, a new pallet is born.

True solitude is not unworthy - it is chosen or placed on you as a sort of new frontier for your species and your individual journey to discover.

If you do not mix well with others or find that your solitude is a sign of your superiority - you are wrong and you are sad inside. Solitude is no privilege or mission. It's only a pallet cleanse of sorts. If you have sadness inside we cannot help you be better or help you feel something - you have to show yourself the way out alone and solitude is a way to do that. It's the untangling via your own wits and the power of creation alone and there is much depth in that passage though it isn't for everyone. Remember, if you feel it's a crime to become close again with other people and you do not look forward to that - your solitude is not good to you. A balance of the mind must be retained.

> "SOLITUDE — A DIP INTO THE OCEAN OF ONENESS."

51
Depression

Depression and other depths.

If you are there – in depth - you might feel a sadness or a numb feeling. Though it feels deep and large, it is actually very finite. Yes, you are there – the one who is sad, but perhaps also energetic enough to feel saintly or melodramatic about it all. There is at least a small immaturity, a little melodrama in every depression cycle. Is it we who do not hold you? We who do not give you the right type of energy or response? Or, is it you that holds yourself tall obeying other worldly impulses and artistic dispositions? Are you the one forever misunderstood?

Well if you're there, oh deep and powerfully eternal one, you are in the wrong. The ethereal realm you are climbing on is not real. The negative perspective on this world will not push you up above other people. There is no dominance in sadness. We are "all-right", we are all just people, and if you can't climb out of your shell with or without us, we do not want you here. The matrix doesn't like you here! Not because we aren't good for you or that we are living in a dark scary unfeeling world, no. We just don't want you if you live in a reality of shadow only, preaching to yourself the comforts that life of shadow holds instead of walking forward with us. If you do not walk forward – you will not be waited for with time.

We don't wait. We are one. Naturally drawn to light and the power of life. Not towards the disregard of it.

Sure there are some individuals that are conditioned well by this world to reach out and help, perhaps some that even create small joys of holding somebody intense, dreamy and inwardly obsessive with great deal of needlessness and need at the same time. It does sound very vampiric and very poetic, but these people aren't well themselves. It all folds in on itself and poof – disappears quickly. No substance met – just lifetimes lost under a shady cloak.

Depth. What is here anyway? Basically a mother or a father wound. Depression is immaturity not a lifestyle! Crawl out of the womb already. Do not confuse your state with any politically correct "humane" perspective on a lengthy disempowering situation. "Ill as part of nature" or "Ill from imposed trauma". You are creator. Get a hold of yourself!

If it's there – inability to withstand darkness - it is not to be revelled in or you will climb into a bad place of ultimate disconnection with all creation with time becoming barely worth a thought. Things that don't grow up grow old quickly. No we do not understand. And no it is not our concern.

We are vibration that is for life. We do not support empty energy signatures.

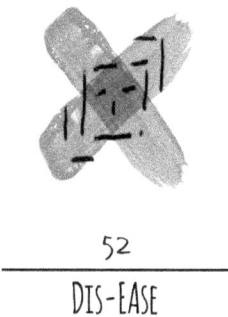

52
DIS-EASE

Not in ease? We don't care if you're sick. No matter the nature of it or the cause - if it's terminal, hereditary, accidental or from birth. Wether we see you on the street, wether we are looking at you on TV or if you are just a relative that's always complaining, we do not care about you and we do not have to. Nobody is carrying you here. People may say they do deeply surrender to the fact that you are not well – but it is all poetry of social misuse of mind. Don't listen to them. We do not care.

It is you with you as the disease within you. This is teaching you or is stimulating you towards being the greater you as nothing else is going to make a change here now.

We do feel you though - that you are here, that you exist, and in that is purpose no matter how well or badly you are feeling. We do want you to be here and we do feel you belong. But, we do not care and in that is great magic (please refer to thoughts on collective conscious at the beginning of the book if in doubt that it's natural for us not to care).

If you are waiting for somebody to truly understand you, expose yourself and your ailment – laugh or cry. Receive the response and be back to where you belong inside, inside yourself. Ask the right questions and wait for the right response. Go within. Sort it out inside. Believe in a future and come back healthy. We believe in you.

53
Prickliness

Is there something on edge right now?

Do you think I'm doing it wrong? Do you think you're doing it wrong? Is this formation – this book or your story somehow not complying with your nature or the way you think is the natural order of things? Are you offended and confused? Good, we have ourselves a prickly one.

Something feels unjust? Is there a pseudo form of political correctness that wants to be involved in getting things "right once and for all"? "The Great Just Being" is just another face of compartmentalization and control, my sweet freedom lover.

Do you have it? That feeling right now? The prickle, the edge?

It may feel fantastic and just, but it won't let you still or move forward past the prickliness. Prickliness makes one stuck and amused with foolish things for too long a time.

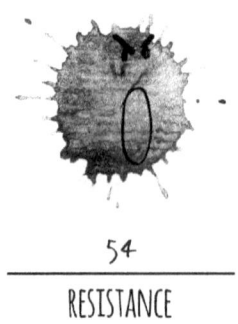

54
Resistance

Do you want to be offered or offended?

Pick one.

Need for justice beyond the world is not bringing in any possibility of expansion. Opportunity quickly comes to those who have an open mind and a tender heart. A tender heart that knows which way to go and where to push without the need for resistance at all. If there is offence, the road is closed, and so is that one. All of them till you "sort it out"…within you or within that which grasps you so much. The tightening of resistance shows in the heart – it prevents new ideas from entering and old ideas from leaving. Everything goes in a circle…. All corrupts and enlightens the feeling of greed for more concern – which is always given more to worry about. In resistance - everything stills without stilling. It stagnates and it can't free.

Resistance may sound poetic but it is not worthy of a cause. It is a worthless time consuming entity that makes one feel empowered for all the stupid reasons. To stand in the face of danger. To stand in the face of politics. Resistance is very stupid but yet somehow poetic and a little bit entertaining for us to watch – so we never say no.

If you offend easily and you resist often, the question lays in the following:

Do you want to "Be"?

55
STAGNANCY

Do you want to be or do you want to dwell?

If you really want to be - keep on choosing yourself with great intensity and emotion within yourself every single day. Nothing else. Don't flake yourself about using your intensity on things that have no true closure or inner most meaning. Political parties. Homes. Situations. People. Ideas. Devotion. All is sickening if your greatest joy and greatest pain comes from the outside world, especially if it's someone else's cause that has nothing to do with you. It just uses you. Like a battery. You will wear your power thin if you don't circulate it within yourself only – by yourself, for the benefit of yourself. All else is futile.

If you did feel something true within, if you did really want to be who you are and take that further, you wouldn't go about stagnating or dwelling on other people's things! If you are dwelling on things, you have a problem. If you are reaching out towards somebody or something – you have a problem. A stagnancy is what puts dis-ease in one's path. Dissatisfaction is what brings about all problems.

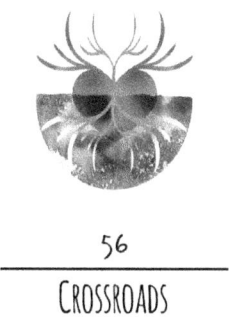

56
CROSSROADS

Are you dissatisfied?

There could be a choice coming on.

Welcome to this part of your journey. Thumbs down? If you are finally here and you feel your worth within utterly and strongly despite what is said or suggested and you feel that the worst is behind you, there is a peak in the distance with your name on it and it has to be something other than this - you are very welcome to do as you please.

If things are getting weird and out of control and you cannot be bothered any longer with this book as a quest let alone with what you have going on in your life – that's good too. Put it down – it means you're done. Don't force anything if you know for a fact you are bored where you are. Do not ever force yourself to commit when you are bored to anything. Boredom is a divine feeling of completion.

Here we are. Here is your stamp of approval from this thought machine and I hope that you have a wonderful day. Enjoy your solutions with pride next time. Welcome to the new phase of your life!

If you are not here yet, you aren't feeling free and you think you're not free there is no conclusion yet. There is resistance still. If you are still on edge and you've got to "do something" but not sure what, please read on dear one even though this book might be wrecking your mind a bit. If there is panic and still uncertainty, well, this book might have some meaning for somebody after all. I'm very happy to see you. You might be lucky in the end because knowledge is power you know…who knows. Maybe you might find some interesting points. Don't change a thing if there is flicker in your energy.

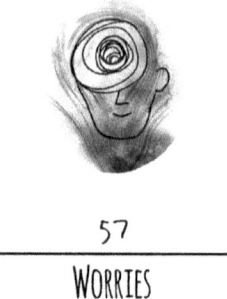

57
Worries

Do you worry? Do you have complaints about your nature, about your world, even about you? Well, my negative friend, if you do complain, you're in the right place, please read on, lets get this on the road.

Do you complain about things at least once a day? Perhaps it's a casual lifestyle choice of sorts. Maybe even a trendy demeanour or style of being.

If that is so, the finger pointing at things, points the other three fingers right back at you. Thrice the complaint is what you receive from reality against what you are. It's a backward little story, but you can't go on forward if you are complaining even about tiny things. Even if your culture or upbringing dictates that a taste of distaste is a sign of culture or some sort of class, there is something wrong here. It isn't cute at all.

Stop the whining, time to get things cleared up. Let's find you amongst it all.

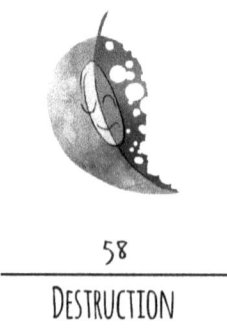

58
Destruction

Self destruction. Destruction of one's storyline.

If you cannot be yourself without complaint, we have a problem on the cards. It's not a good one, it's not an easy one. It's a bad one.

If we have somebody concerned and disconnected with themselves at the same time, we have a person who's not able to be a well rounded, naturally feeling person. This may not be obvious as they may feel that they try or that they truly care. Imagine an avalanche of care or a tornado of deep need….it's not easy and it isn't tolerated by this reality often. There is a part of a destructive human being that knows that they are not welcome though, which makes it even harder to end the cycle of destroying things.

If you have to try hard to be positive outwardly no matter what is going on inside, or if you try to be that special something you're not in order to be "allowed to be" we have an addiction of sorts on our hands. Destructiveness is an addiction to a lower standard of self awareness and that is hard to shift without understanding what is behind it. Until you see the true face of what you're dealing with beyond the mask of virtue and pleasantries you might not stand a chance to understand how to shift it! To understand this phenomenon, please read on through the next few thoughts.

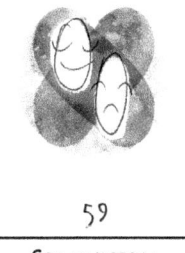

59

Compulsion

Being there. No matter what! A.K.A - Loyalty beyond self.

So…are you that girl – the one who's always the bridesmaid but never the bride? Are you the fellow that is in the friend zone for eternity desperately seeking a mate? Are you a confused, deluded human being who thinks nobody wants it the way you do and you've got to play along forever no matter what? Perhaps life has dealt you a hand and you feel that is the only way for you here? The way of compromise and stealth - a silent, still, intense way of life beyond the curtain, in the background, behind someone else's dream?

Or are you making it to the foreground finally, still considering yourself unremarkable somehow?

Is your way of life slower than you feel it should be or is there constant messages from "god" that things aren't good in your neighbourhood?

Stop Compulsive Life Choices.

Get new friends, get out, stop staring, start thinking straight!!

When you finally do let yourself shed that weight of loyalty and worship, trust is shortly replaced by ownership beyond control. Watch it glow and shift shape. The pure hearted person behind the scenes suddenly becomes a silent criminal. The gorgeous friend who's never happy for herself as much as her friends usually becomes a psychopath. It is underneath. It is waiting and it should never have to surface – should you discover…

A new life grid is more than important than compulsive behaviour that doesn't fit with your natural instincts.

It's not easy to be this way. We appreciate it. Just trust that those people, cultural trends, aspects of your reality or paths you are servicing out of inner guilt aren't worth a thing. You are "it". You always have been. Start your own games and be who you are.

60

RAGE

Rage

You get raged up? You think you have fire and strength? Think again…

Rage is actually a sign of submission. It shows inconsistency and inability to be proudly awake and here. In rage, the fire in you can't flow through your veins in careless cool swirly style that signifies maturity. True fire is productive. It is worthy, it is warm.

Rage just means that your inner fire has to be a showy phenomenon that gushes, protrudes, flickers untamed just to show itself off or to feel that it is there. Have you got flickers of fire within? You're a weak person no matter how big or muscular you may seem. It is not sensational, it isn't proud. Fire within that flickers isn't mature. It is weakness parading as strength. Sort it out – see it's true colours.

61
PASSION

Lots of fire is passion, no? Well yes...but no. No my friend, no.

Mature passion summoned for greater joy and creation pulls in as a deep swirl of sturdy syrupy flow. Just like a man with a good understanding of his erection, steady passion can create beautifully and reach well timed, great inner mastery. Enjoy it in useful doses with great loyalty to self and deep intention of the dreamer.

Passion is a timed and abundant purifying vortex of inner knowledge. It isn't sickly, it doesn't yelp or howl. It transforms.

If you are gushy and rocky like a puppy learning to bark that is not true passion. It's an energy scatter. Pushiness doesn't vibrate or resonate as power. It is unfortunate and annoying sometimes like a gust of cold air in a comfortable room. Control these gusts of devotion, they bring you trouble and us – unnecessary concerns and un-nurtured feelings.

In the case of the untamed passion - growing up is in order. It is a nice profound step that is always necessary. If one has no energetic mastery, the gush of what parades as genuine passion isn't understood or mastered. Un-mastered passion is scattered and so is this lifetime. Manifestation is finite and unbalanced for someone who is pushy without steady flow. Children that come into life through such passion weak or dosed with constant grief. Without self mastery and inner value, one is not in range of oneself. Something always folds or falls short as energy is not maintained in a steady stream. Passionate people who cannot pull themselves together are often loved, but yet are stuck without noticing they are in a constant energetic nightmare addicted to what they provide another or how their energy shifts for it's own delight. Such playfulness with one's own passion doesn't bring true knowledge, self discipline or understanding of value. Wake up to this treadmill of unbalanced energy one might call "passion". Still. If you can't wake up or still - complain. (read thoughts from number 53 onwards again).

See the child in you before you see the adult. Try to work it out with that inner child in some way first before scattering yourself. Without the help of that inner child - you can never grow up. Feel what they have to say to you inside and nurture that connection deeply, eventually becoming your own parent, through which you may understand the value of your life and the abundant energy that is given to you for great purpose not for scatter.

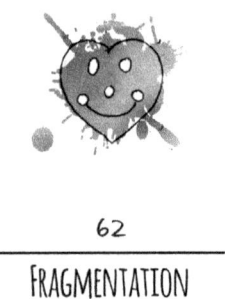

62
FRAGMENTATION

Fragmentation is illusive. It can come on strong often when we don't care to see it or are awake enough to identify it.

Picture this – a meek demeanour with no timeline, place or gender. An ambiguous space, with not a worry in the world! Suddenly the grown man or woman may seem wide eyed and excited about life like a little child, there might be beauty everywhere yet use of nothing made – and that we see as innocent and pure. Surprisingly it is not what it seems. It is a form of escapism from reality through the fragmentation of one's ego which isn't sweet at all.

What is there? Just an innocent little voice inside, a sweet little being comes out sometimes wishing all to surrender to simple joy – all bow to the beauty of the innocent little child within. The "inner voice". The "inner child". How beautiful. No.

Children are good, so why not become one again? The ageless beautiful wide eyed girl or boy. The good kid inside of you that feels it wouldn't betray, it wouldn't give up and it definitely wouldn't lie or steal. Well, the thing it is hiding is that

It would do all those terrible things. It is why this fragmentation is here.

The fragmentation you glorify as a very nice and neatly surprising special part of you is actually not what it seems. It's a fault of yours that you can't consider yet as a part of your reality in all sufficiency and human embodiment. What then?

Through the whimsical creature of escapist joy, insufficiency knocks on your door through time and space from a time when you were very young – an old trauma parading as a gift of sorts. You utilize it, glorify it maybe, inviting it, wanting it to be there all the time maybe, but what is it in the funny little inner child that's not true? It's not you. That's what. You are not the energy of yourself aged 6 anymore and that will never change. Combining with the energy of the inner child isn't going to give you anything. It is not pure and it is not ageless. It's escapist and it will not heal a thing without you catching up to your own biological reality.

The inner child syndrome is deep need to never be responsible and to never have done wrong. It is the worst case of escapism. It is an indicator of intense grief and often shame.

What does this curious character give of? Trauma because from trauma it has come. The Peter Pan! Miss Tinker Bell! Let them fly off and not come back. They aren't you anymore. Perhaps they never even were. There is no need to hold these behaviours close – they cannot feed and they do not allow progress to happen.

Take back all you have given yourself through the inner child obsession that is not constructive to your "normal life" – all those toys, those blankets, those specialty items, the emotional crutches that you may have made out of people and yes the deep need to be held and adored. It is emotional clutter. All of this isn't for you to grow or develop. It is not healthy and it cannot stay.

The inner child is recited often, sometimes paraded, sometimes hidden depending often on the parent's values in childhood. The funny thing is that the inner child syndrome holds the biggest key to you imaginable, but it won't give it up unless you learn to deal with it and parent your own self entirely. If out of hand, the inner child gets mistaken for an integral part of you, an angelic part of you, even mistaken for the true expression of your soul. Sometimes it is strong enough run people's lives for them. It can really give a lot and take even more, but the personal story often stays the same, and yes, it does dement you in older years if you do not know how to give yourself the opportunity to make it your friend, create for it a portal and connect to it seamlessly. In close proximity – this fragmentation system cannot stay. It will dissolve or disappear as it should have a long time ago perhaps, but not until you put in the work. If you identify it correctly perhaps you are half way there.

If your "inner child" isn't you, then what is it exactly?...

> "THE INNER CHILD POWERED REALITY IS ESCAPIST. IT WILL NOT HEAL A THING WITHOUT YOU CATCHING UP TO YOUR CURRENT BIOLOGICAL REALITY."

63
ENTITIES

Demons, entities and spirits.

That's right. We've all got them to an extent and we do not like to understand that. We are conditioned to be afraid, that is why, though in the end, they are all an integral part of the great design of this world. They are an emotional crutch when we need it and a best friend when we think that isolation is a possibility. They nurture and teach us but in time, yes, like old props they must be ascended through as they too must themselves ascend and not loiter for too long a time.

We don't like the idea of dark spirits. We hate the idea. We discard it with fear and disgust. We don't like to know that something else is working through us sometimes let alone watches us or powers us. We get told to just "stay away" to "pull ourselves out" but we cannot bring ourselves to creation without shadow too so we must take them on. We must conquer that piece of us that is afraid – not the demon or dark energy. Just ourselves. We must not be afraid – that's the main cause of them being in contact with us. They are only the symptom of a discontent feeling that we have inside. We harbour the feeling – they show up. It is easy. We start something badly – they show up. We entrap our minds and hearts – they are there. It is that easy. As if by lightning, they are there as soon as we are off our track emotionally or energetically.

Quite commonly through the most virtuous people works the darkest energy. How do you navigate through this pickle then? Well, do you have a split personality? Do you sometimes go out the window and a part of you can't stop or can't start something? Does something accentuate suddenly and you have yourself an alter ego or the "confident you"? The "other self". The "predominant one" or the "extra quiet one". Do you auto pilot often? If yes, we have something to be ridding you of here. Don't be afraid. That's the point.

Yes there are many ways through depth and trauma or deep need and commitment to life and God that can indeed help. However, it is not for everyone to do things quickly as most people under current cultural conditioning cannot fathom an exorcism or a deep gush of the soul, then what? What to do? Ayahuasca is a choice. Extreme prayer is a choice. But what if it's not easy to imagine?

Read the next few chapters.

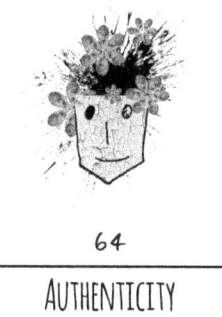

64
AUTHENTICITY

Be you. Yes, you. That is all you need.

Don't hide behind a mask or a demeanour that is actually a demon or entity inside. Does an inner spiritual or emotional condition "make you" do this or that? Do you act different under certain circumstance or in a certain light? If you do, and especially if you use that energy to seduce, reflect and "mean something" more than just you being you, we have a problem. If it feels like you sometimes but not you consistently, rid of that shell – rid of that entity. Just say no.

Be you. Explore what that means in primal ways, in physical ways, in natural ways:

What are your arms saying about you? What is your voice truly? How does it ring? What is it that it wants to say half the time? What is that stomach? What is that body? What are your eyes saying every day? How is it all sitting? What is perhaps the comment from another about you? What is the most consistent comment that you receive from strangers? E.g. "you are gorgeous", "you look tired", "you are insane" - what is that energy that you do not feel understood in? What is the problem? What is that? Explore the basic parameters of your being.

Start there. Radiate out from what you do have physically and tangibly and what you truly are. Start in the body, radiate out.

Don't go chasing shadows or any ill. Stop your work or your programs if you do not know who you are or what is powering you. Stop all debris in the face of social media and polluting communication. Stop it all. Listen inside.

.....

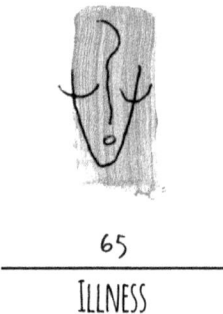

65
ILLNESS

If you do not think you are well and you feel you might have something very, very weird or ill about you - think again. There might be a need to be ill. In that case reconsider right here, Do not read the rest of this chapter.

You may think you aren't well because you know you've got to do a lot to get to the top of you. You see yourself – the self that should have been perhaps as sort of a mount everst perhaps – you see that you've gone too far astray and there's a lot to do now to get yourself to centre.

You see it, can't you – the divide between you and the person that you may have become – you know you have to start getting yourself back, that's fine. You are welcomed by life if you want to travel back to self and get back on track. Always. if you do understand that becoming well is your own personal journey, we will aid you. You will be given. Being ill as a lifestyle is a label that you can indeed hand over to yourself and be at peace with that – that is true, but can you?

Can you achieve peace with the label of illness beyond this world? Can you not feel bad for not trying? Do you want it to continue? Do you want to be this person who is lost and will start a new cycle after this one again and again lost or confused about something?

No. It's not human to want to be this.

So don't hand yourself that label. The sick for life label. Think again. Keep on changing, change and evolve. That is the only way from it. Be strong and be at peace only when you know you have done great deeds and work on yourself - the light of your lifetime is poised, loved and evolved. In journey is your portal now if you are truly ill. Don't be afraid. There is no karma.

66
Mastery

Yes, mastery. How nice a word. The long hard yards of the human evolution spectrum. Endless, right? Up the mountain to the guru. All the way up…wait a minute…

Where are you? Do you think you're evolved? Do you think you're not? You're going to get there? Is it far to go yet? Is this mountain high enough or low enough?

It's hard to chase mastery. Nobody succeeds.

Are you walking?

Just walk. Just be.

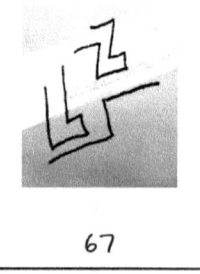

67
Progress

Are you winning? Offcourse - over something else? Are you ascending or heightening? Can you feel it?

Progress is funny. It is a gradual process not a leap out of nowhere and is best achieved unconsciously! You are constantly moving up you know. Spiralling as is all life. You are always evolving. Are you not? Do you feel you are welcoming change and shift each day? Do you feel welcoming of life to take it's creative right in your experience and you feel completely un-phased by it all – just soaking up the beauty of the moment?

Yes? Then you are progressing AUTOMATICALLY

No? You're not in your body? Well?

Start walking. All is inside you. Not in a virtual game with life.

Fun fact – the less you place attention on attainment and progress the less likely you are to experience stagnation. The less you think about it all the more it happens on it's own. Automatic progress is not impossible – allowing for it is allowing nature to take it's turn. It's the non-resistance way to great change.

Plants and children grow best when you don't watch the grow.

68
Inversion

Immerse inside you, be within you no matter what – this is the only lifetime you'll get being "this version of you" – soak it up!

Are you inside or on the outside of you? That's the simple question. If you are inside, you can feel yourself circulating within, you're good. If you're not feeling it, if you are out there somewhere getting information and sensation from outside not within, get inside you! Why?

It's all about you baby.

This whole lifetime of yours is about "how to get into you more and be more like you" That is a success story right there. Circulate internally. Become the process of all life inside – become the galaxy - start it now - inside! If you can, stop thinking about what you do and do not want to be and understand that which you are right now. Refine it in time perhaps, but for now just trust it, exactly where you are, as you are.

Savour this version of you in the eternal moment of pleasure – it will change your world.

Trust. Yourself.

Every cell as it is. Every grey hair is perfection right now. Every wrinkle, pimple or inconsistency of any part of you. Start there. And be. Learn to be you as you are. And breathe.

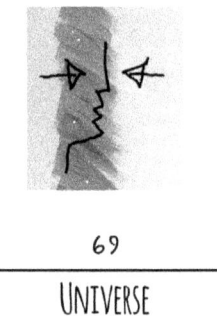

69

Universe

Being inside you. You - the universe in human form are already complete just as you. You are all you need in this younivserse as it is deeply you. The younivserse is a giant human after all, and you my friend are part of it all. Perhaps you are it all.

That's right it doesn't stop with acceptance. You accept that you are well – that is great, but you have to start walking forward. You have to start being, doing and protruding as you while not scattering any of your energy too. Be mindful of your time here – it is magic!

If you are questioning always and you aren't certain in the centre that you yourself are able to provide yourself, that is not bad! Do you ask yourself: "What is it? This whole purpose thing? What is it being human? Why are we here?"

You are not content in your own universe. That's ok and you were chosen not to be content for a very special reason – if you ask all the questions, you are elevating the rest of us to know something better!

Let's start there then – uncertainty….please read on.

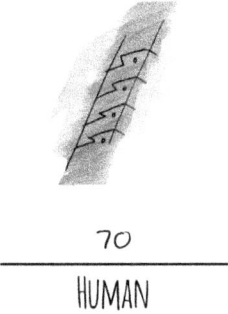

70
HUMAN

Human. Let's remind us what that means.

You are a relatively small mammal that stands on two hind legs. Hopefully. If you don't yet do that, it's ok. We'll fix you!

Wether or not your legs are available, you are a mammal designed to embody itself, to congregate, to enjoy, move and shake through motion, through plasma in your veins and an intense deep feeling that we associate with psychosis on this planet which is actually rapture. Is that scary? No, that's just you. It's your nature to be very sensitive and a little chaotic. A bit fragile and a tiny bit insane unlike (or seemingly unlike) anyone you know or would ever know. That's the basic human blueprint there. It's all the same for everyone.

Human. You are not being human if you aren't going places - that's not just a superficial statement about climbing corporate scales or hierarchical pyramids of any sorts though for some mountain goats it's fun. We're not talking metaphorically here, no.

If you aren't walking, shifting changing space and looking for more, you aren't exploring this amazing world where all is possible - you aren't human. You've become just a hmmmm…..

Start your moving, start your shaking, begin!

"SAVOUR THIS VERSION OF YOU IN THE ETERNAL MOMENT OF PLEASURE — IT WILL CHANGE YOUR WORLD!"

71
Inspiration

Can't decide what you're up to? Can't decide where you're going? Hmmm. Human you have work to do.

Decide now – who you are. Quick! Think the first thing! (a flash is all that's needed for some) Otherwise if you are extra choosy, give yourself some time, stop reading here…. STOP….think.

OK good the first flash is usually the best, for some it takes a while but information is always available and yes, inspiration is always on the go! Don't worry if it wasn't good or real for you yet, if it didn't feel necessary or strong yet, just stay with that first initial impression. For now. You don't have to know it inside out – who you are straight away if you're still in a state of "hmmm". It's ok if you don't know. Trust what you do know so far, go with that and you will succeed because the greater the urge to move and shift – the bigger the openness towards greater outcomes outcome. Start walking towards what you "kind of" understand for now, the bigger picture will expand itself in front of you. The more you delve and pry into inspiration the more it is likely to humour and play without confusion.

Just like walking through a landscape yet unseen. Trust. Enjoy. Play. All will be revealed.

"BE LED BY YOUR IMPULSE TODAY – MAKE YOUR DREAMS COME TRUE TOMORROW!"

72
Impulse

Be that which feels good right now.

Right now. Not forever…just right now. For you. Just for you. Just like that. Be led by your impulse today – make your dreams come true tomorrow. Nothing to worry about. If you don't have a clear impulse about who you are – if you are still in the past, carefully planning the future, you are stuck. We need to get your impulse back in line! And we have to nurture it as a normal part of your world again where it belongs! Zzzap!

Does it feel good to go clubbing and get together with somebody or do any other weirdly immature and compulsive feeling thing? Just now? Well, maybe it's not something to commit to you forever, but know it's not about that. It's about clearing your pallet for more fun. So if you say, wanted to do it for ages but the impulse just got inward, built up and stale - you have lost yourself. So take the plunge - go for it!

When we have pent up impulse from years ago our dreams don't generate quickly and easily – that is because we have stuck it out somewhere we didn't want to be when it was time to move shake and shiver! Perhaps it is now that you are worried about your impulses as you have come to know that often yes – they are compulsive and sometimes even repulsive to you let alone to another! But – the longer you wait the more likely you are to become deeply stuck. The clarity of your pallet is a must if you do not want to use your impulse anymore. Lets adjust it right here – think of what you want to do or experience and do it straight away (within reason) – see how easy it is to do small things? Then big things won't be so hard. Sure, often these impulses are very immature and strange if we have been bottling them up for a while – but they have to come loose, come clean and come away to enrich us with greater meaning and stronger, wiser impulses in the future.

Get it all out of your system at least on some wavelength. Would it feel good to sit still and read the bible right now? To read, to write to draw, to process? Boring perhaps. That's fine. If it's an impulse by now, that's great – it is the way your cookie crumbles - do that. You've been conditioned to study. That's powerful too. Follow that if it's an actual pleasure based impulse. Do it. That's fine. See what comes of it. See if it will fold and flow in other forms maybe with time or if it opens to a greater need to merge energetically or physically again!

If you would like to know more about you, if you would really like to master you, then don't waste your time thinking, timing and feeling. That will take forever to uncover the truth behind you. Want to know you right now? Hear your impulse. Just to clarify and see yourself honestly, a good impulse is always stimulating and very uniquely yours. What is beneath the action and the impulse anyway? You won't find out clearly through speculation. It is in the doing that the story is revealed and that part of you that is yet curious and unnourished can ascend!

The quicker the impulse the better and the healthier for you – otherwise you stagnate, hibernate and harbour all sorts of things even if you think that you're moving forward in some practical or social way.

Got the idea? Start. Impulse! Zzzap!

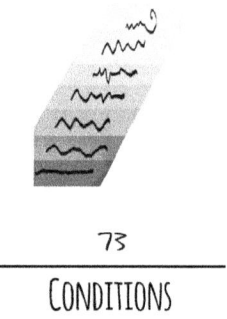

73
_____
Conditions

We create conditions for ourselves that we feel we cannot overcome often or barriers that we feel stand in between us and that something else. "But…I can't do it!" - sounds familiar to most of us.

Conditions create a conditional lifetime in a surprisingly unconditional universe. That is the irony that we have been living for a long time as a species now. Conditions rule us and in that way make us triumphant over very little we feel. In the end it is the condition that wins not the human as we are constantly reminded by this system where we belong it is all beyond us and that only in servicing others can we find space for ourselves. We somehow try to appease conditions always and that is hard to live with. What now?

Well, you've got to bring it all back to you. An impulse creates itself divinely and automatically for you to follow through with pride and clarity. Without censorship hopefully just to get yourself through into the next frontier of personal human evolution. It doesn't matter if it is good or bad – the outcome or the deed. You just have to follow through. Impulse may seem meek or strong, good or bad, powerful or weak – but the main purpose of impulse is pride in yourself – the ability to go forward, the stamina and the strength that is needed to create a much bigger portal for your soul to experience, a huge catalyst maybe for some, a steady road for others.

Take the first step.

You don't have to begin to be a famous traveller if you are just starting out thinking about where you'd like to be yet. You can just go out every day to the dock and sit by the same water every day just to get a taste for the dream of travel. Don't stay inside. Or do, but read an atlas, or meet somebody online from a different continent to you. If you don't want to write just yet that is fine, share your thoughts with people in other ways. Just do the equivalent of what you think you are now in ability of. Do the equivalent of what you want to be on a smaller scale perhaps just yet – do whatever is believable to you now - greater self belief will come.

As above so bellow, there is no big or small, aren't we just fractal beings after all! Believe. Miracles happen fast! End result feels simple and easy to see – like magic, though often the first step of the pinnacle at some point seemed a miracle. A simple step seemed a lifetime. It's ok. Just take the first step.

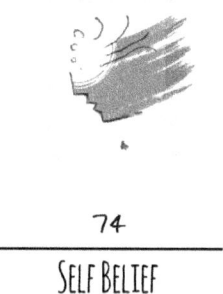

74

Self Belief

What is self belief anyway? Why is it a problem? If you do not believe in you – that would mean that you aren't, and if you are not, then what are you?? If you don't believe you are, you better sit down for this. Or maybe even lye down.

Your identity as a human being is lost.

It is hard when you aren't able to truly be embodied or even be in ways present to this experience. It is not as uncommon as it should be. It will not be hard to understand after you read the following chapters, but here is a clue for you now.

Do not condescend yourself ever. If you do – you are likely going to hide from yourself forever.

Humour and light hearted approach is one thing. Condescending of yourself is another. If you cannot be really present to anything or anyone that you have been or done in the past – you need inertia to kick into you again. You need to belt out what you deeply want and need – what you desire and what this all has been coming to. If the energy of passion seems strong or too bolshy to express- we are in trouble here. As I was only two years ago.

You have to do a lot of work to grasp that you are here which would need to be a process of re-identification of you all together. Don't worry. We'll get you through together!

If you do not feel you are or do not think you are - you're very stuck! We have to get you out through some creative reprogramming, please read on.

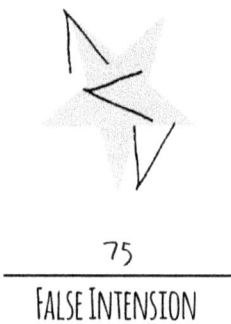

75
False Intension

Conceptualization. The unmade, the badly understood. Thought over matter. Concept over real life. Abstract Intention. Fluffery, fakery and other concepts of "truth" beyond experience. Welcome to the underworld where intellectualization of all things brings nothing good, but yet perhaps generates a lot of free flow and banter in the process of clouding everybody's mind. Not so nice.

"What is conceptual and what is real anyway?" You might ask. "Isn't this just a dry quantum world?" No.

How about your life, a life that's not just a concept. Would it important to only live for a day or if you didn't come into existence at all? Just a concept inside your mother's thoughts. Would that be well? Or would that be strange?

No matter your unique and sincere concept of reality – you are here - you are, this is – it exists. Please consider the realistic 3D parameters of your reality, your body and the grid of this planet, lets get right down to basics. There's no other way.

Do you consider yourself a creative in any sense? Good.

Are you creating all day every day or often at least? Good - that is a journey, a practice. A truth. Your concepts are alive or are in vortex. That is clear. If you see your timeline change drastically or you see your world shift? That's even better. Are you able to make something for us we haven't yet experienced? Great. Does there seem to be appreciation and creative generation in other people? Great – keep going with it for the while.

Are you one of those bright individuals who just receives praise by knowing the right people, clicks or popular things to say?? That's fine. But is it creation? No. It is salesmanship of a concept - so are you an artist? In a way. A con artist. Not a real creator. Your creation is void of meaning, it isn't real. You are conceptually creative perhaps, but a true creator you are not unless you create the concept for the purpose of it's achievement.

Are you trying to navigate a concept without making any practical steps or having it as an internal journey? Is it sitting forever on the shelf dusting away like an old trophy or is it splashed around senselessly for the need to be perceived as something? If you are trying to understand life or live deeply without actually putting your body through things - creativity is impossible. Without practice or without manifestation, a concept is just a concept – an empty world. An ethereal energy that hardly can stand itself let alone stand it's purpose. Unloved, unused and unexpanded concepts become part of the scrap me(n)tal of the ethereal collective mind. It's just that. Ethereal (s)crap.

If you however do have concepts, and in some way you live them or breathe them into existence, what you are is not a conceptual person and you will not create in vain. You may not receive what you thought would be best for what you do every time but the creation or the connection of a concept into physical existence or tangible means is useful beyond words. No full blooded creation or experience is in vain. It is learning, it is study, it is life.

Your concept and your realness it is in many ways you, and you become more as your creative concepts with time. If you are flapping your gums about concepts you aren't embodying, loving or truly living, you aren't here my friend. You're in the abyss. Carry yourself through what you preach. Practice it. Make it real.

If you just want to talk about it and not create it or not to see it live – that is hard to face but you are creating something you do not want to be embodied. That is the trouble here. There is no trust of you or it to be. There is need for spiritual or emotional cleansing there.

If you don't carry through what you've come to create, it absorbs you.

....

76
MIRACLE

A paradigm shift is in order If you will…

Here – right here if you like, we are lucky enough to have a window for you to shift.

You can move on through it. Right now. Miracles can be.

Only if you want to.

It is up to you – define it as you will - be the shift by allowing shift as a miraculous possibility! This paradigm shift window is real, but also is not real – it is conceptual. Can you feel it? Do you believe it? If you do believe it's possible - it is yours.

If you do not believe it is possible to shift paradigms swiftly, what is the purpose of this disbelief? What is the struggle? Why can't you shift into miracle space yet?

Because you aren't creative enough. You're just intellectually conceptual without ability to leave room for a miracle. Leave your mind for once, allow the mindless miracle to just be. Let God drive. Allow it. Believe it as so. This will heal your mind from non creative outcomes in the future.

All life is miracle. All life is. That which wasn't before possible is possible now. All that exists now was once reliant on a miracle of sorts to alchemise itself. We are all walking miracles and that which we do and create is a miracle too. You are miracle. Why would a miracle be beyond you?

If you aren't accustomed to the reality of miracles or if you aren't making the miracle justifiable to yourself in your mind through work and perseverance or even prayer, it's hard to generate these paradigm shifts. Combination of prayer and work does makes all things possible.

What to do if there is not a part of you that wants to put in the energy that makes the shift plausible or trust enough to believe that the shift is real? What is it that is unable to be undone enough to allow God to drive? Obsession with fact, purpose, need for understanding. Lack of trust. Deep control of one's own mind. Grasp on reality that will not generate anything new anymore as the mind is too made up already to let possibility be a factor. In other words:

Illusion.

77
Illusion

Are you in lala land? Do you collect useful and useless information fragments of reality and experience for a silly purpose? Do you like to simply flash your "knowledge" or "wisdom" in front yourself or worse – other people - to distract you from your life? Maybe even connecting to a little gang of people that also like to know their facts "just so"?

Do you spend too much time in alternate realities that do not bring clear perspective? Do you like long walks along quantum beach under the starry eyed sky, enjoying a very particularly created version of yourself and this universe that is shrouded in multiplicity and intricacy, yet nothing makes much sense? Do you have your own special brand of the unreal? Are you swallowing too many pills or living a life of habit and addiction both ethereal or physical?

Stop that fluffery. You are fluffing with the wrong things my dear.

It may seem enticing, poetic and just, and yes, we have all been there even though you might not think we are as special as you. Stop pushing illusion of your life before the physical or the obvious principals that are shared by everyone else's story. Don't distort or contort yourself and other people to fit your principals of reality. Yes it is unusual, but not useful. We are all awakened beings in some sense, we know everything and yes, mostly on the unconscious level. We are tied together by very simple facts of life. If you do not believe that we are truthful – we are. We are simple beings. We just need to know you as one of us – not one of the "other kind" that you imagine.

As you follow your road through illusion continuously, there is not a lot of interest that we with time can hold for you. As one becomes an illusion addict we give up on wanting to help you understand something bigger, something brighter – us. You. The world. We give up. It is a lonely road if you remain sleeping and yes, a terrible ending perhaps as those who have not heeded to the real and the living for fear of loss of their illusionary worlds, often have a strange voyage by the time they are ready to leave this place to karmically make up for their strange innuendos and unnatural scenarios. It is not easy.

Shed energy that you do not need to entertain, shed all illusion, romance with the shadow or the light, all that junk. It will not do you any justice in the end. Illusionary worlds is not why you are born human.

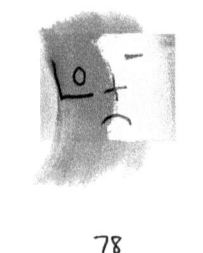

78
False Value

Special – not special…

Are you or aren't you then?

And who is the judge?

You? Do you understand that if it is others that you claim to judge you, it is still you that is judging?

If you are sure that you have nothing to do with judgement, though there's often others pointing finger at your elevation or depravation - that's very bad. If you think there's another person or people that are pointing their finger, or maybe there are some special beings or God doing that, you have to start thinking and understanding the world better my friend. Maybe you need to go through some depth or introversion in order to understand what you are – feel and realise that you are inseparable from people. Understand eventually maybe that people are not at all separate aspects, especially the people that catch your attention. They are just you in a separate body, acting as a "separate" force while being intricately…you. We're all one being. We are you.

If you understand that it is you that is judging you, that's a good place to be for now....if you are the judge of yourself - can you please judge yourself sincerely and tell yourself all of it? Get it out of your system quickly as all external judgement chatter is leading back to you. It isn't kind neither is it structural usually, just a bunch of loops that are well ironed over. This is nothing to revel in. It's a waste of your time.

If you struggle with your judgement based patterns - make a judgement day or the day of the reveal. Become the statue of liberty for just one day – tell you what you feel in great detail. Make it an occasion to really go for it. Rip into who you are with force. Spend the whole day wining and dining your ego through an inner divorce, and make sure to enjoy each step of the way – as if you are both the big boss and the servant. Indulge and enjoy the ability to call the shots and point the finger. No longer than one day though, and maybe your head will come out of your butt as you merge some polarities, maybe you might light up and understand something there, maybe you won't.

It would be fun to see, and should eventually offcourse - dissolve in laughter.

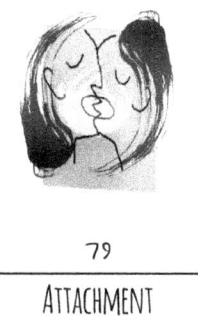

79
Attachment

Attachment to another. Attachment to a part of you. Any attachment.

Are your friends not sincere with you? Do you feel afraid or unwell in them somehow? Do you feel that they will not or never really will be there for the best reasons? Will they be there? Will they not be there? Is there speculation and constant fluctuation in your trust for this world and maybe your trust of self?

That is great breeding ground for any types of attachments.

Will others get the greater concept you bring into this world? Will they merge with you completely? Is there a family possible or a marriage? Will this thing that you are doing bring some part of you to a greatness and a feeling of completion? Do you think about it? Do you want a serene ideal with yourself or other people?

This is loss. Attachment is a human need to be at a loss unconsciously. It is what brings about the much needed perhaps disconnection, the needed proof that yes you are indeed alone. It has to happen. You are asking for it unconsciously if you attach.

A life of attachments is a life down the toilet.

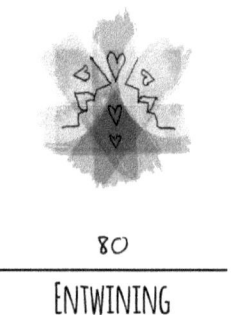

80
ENTWINING

Wanting to be with something, to become something through another or be entwined with someone for a very long time?

This is a bit out of line. It is using your time here unjustly or even unnecessarily and it does hurt.

Are you needlessly pulling yourself into something or somebody? Is it that magnetic pull that is sucking you into another aspect of you through another thing or person?

Get out of this vibration – that feeling is false. Deep infatuation or entwining is possession at it's worst.

And not just that, It's a waste of love and light on something that's not even an illusion. It's a dependency or a destiny warp, where you cannot go forward with ease and natural self efficient flow. Under possession of an artificial obsession or plan, you create a roundy-bouty road for you to travel in low efficiency, not getting to the point that you need for a very long time perhaps. This road won't bring about the straight forward choices or straight forward manifestation, as the road is between two things that are not merging – because no atoms are made to merge. No people are halves to each other.

To be oneself in the face of love of another is a choice and an unawakened one when ready. Being attached to a concept or a person makes it impossible to have balance and creates deep dormancy.

We are not suggested that sovereignty is empowering by our social systems because it is too empowering to do so!

We are asked instead to merge constantly through the different mediums available to us. Through music, through screen play – we are asked constantly to merge with something or somebody by mainstream society. It's not seen as normal to be disconnected from everyone in our choices, to be sovereign to our own inner worlds. Yes - we are all one, and yes alone and together in all ways. We do not need to entice one another to merge closer – there is no merging already – we are love. To entice greater merging between people with no boundaries is absurd – being you beyond all other factors is your purpose here. Your true human purpose is inside, always is always was. It is through inner joy and pain, not with anything or anyone else in perspective beyond you that you merge deeper…with you! People are a factor offcourse and often they aid, but as all learning aids, they fall off into their own creative flow. Everything ends, all envy, all need and all karma that comes with merging too. What stays? You do. The soul. Being moulded and shifted around by others, nothing more.

If you are clinging - you're pushing your own impulse, your own soul backwards into itself relying on disillusionment and trauma to grow unconsciously and become heavy enough to burst you open. Merging a rocky, rocky road. It's unnecessary. It is not as beautiful as it seems.

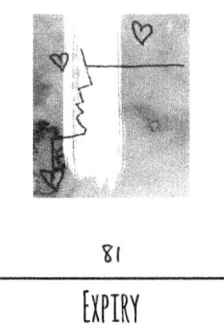

81

Expiry

Don't worry. Expiry is a regular part of life in the works with all things constantly on some level. Everything constantly regrows and yes in order to grow – expires too.

Just like the natural eco system of the forest or the garden – expired plants provide more to the living ones. Expiry allows things to naturally fold in such a way all to bring new life again, and yes, a new death once more.

Whatever you are clinging to still – be it a job or a person, will not be there for long. Even in perfect love and marriage there are scientifically proven periods of energetic expiry. This is because the mind cannot any longer generate the same concepts or chemicals after certain periods. The flow of energy just expires. It intersects and it runs dry. Some say 2, some say 7 years is it. That first emotion, that initial big bang between people just gets up and walks away.

This is not surprising since our bodies do change completely every 7 years. It would be almost impossible to radiate compatible chemistry on all levels throughout any long term relationship.

All is a journey of combination and separation. It's always this way with reality.

Some say that the most unconditional love is that of a parent and it lasts lifetimes.

But watch what happens with parents too - they are treating you differently now that you're a different age, and they did truly love you so, so, so much. It is the brightest star of love for most people – birthing their own child. But mostly, these stars fade away too.

When the relationship hits the expiry point - whatever is left behind in the lasting relationships chemically and energetically is a sort of husk of feelings and unexplored potential, perhaps guilt and the remaining un-useful behaviours. You wake up to this expiry and amaze to see that there was nothing holy or deep in the end. The dream is over.

If you are engaged in a soul union of any type, just surrender to the system of each other – an evolution that is distilled between the two parties. A growing together of sorts in a very timeless, strong bind, which is eventually recognised as uninteresting and lifeless by many unless they are constantly growing and changing for themselves only. Or if there are very intense factors in that timeline.

Being with another for a long time is a process of re-evaluating self worth, not the process of commitment.

And yes in your marriage - I do not doubt it's a success – there is little possibility for unity. And that is fact. It's very rare and if it happens – unnatural - to grow forward in alignment. Even though there maybe is room to progress together, a race to run along each other, but nothing lasts when we rely on each other. There is a sort of inner commerce involved there. When we notice interdependency and a sort of self feeding through another person - a fading in the works. Expiry has come.

If you are there in the process of expiry right now and you are worried about it - don't. It was timed from the basis of "eternity" when nothing can truly immortal but your own energy. That which beckons with forever is bound to fail and open your eyes deeper into yourself. Your own forever, your own eternal moment inside. Off with the training wheels.

That is that.

"EXPIRY IS A REGULAR PART OF LIFE"

82

Bliss

Bliss is not quite bliss if it is created by something or someone else. It's an interesting feeling but bliss it cannot be. If you are able to generate bliss within with nobody around and nothing specifically to stimulate you, you're onto something amazing! Bliss isn't created it is explored within. Bliss is available always, it is inside yourself, always has been, always will be.

If bliss is harder and harder with age to pull in, you're not in the right dimension there. Bliss isn't pulled in. It's generated through all space and time within.

If you do not enjoy yourself in any way and you don't do it often for yourself alone, you are ageing in the worst way – you are being held lower than you need to by your understanding of yourself. You pull yourself down.

If you are a burden to yourself you are a burden to all people.

If you are here – burdened by you - stay that way. Maybe if you are heavy enough one day that energy will fold, something will let go and you'll flow again….It's something that happens over time if a burden of self is created. It has to ripen and break, kind of like a breaking of water or the falling of fruit. Perhaps then you will become more aware through your own self rebirth.

Carry yourself, care for yourself, break free, be reborn into purity and bliss.

"BLISS ISN'T CREATED, IT IS EXPLORED WITHIN. BLISS IS AVAILABLE ALWAYS, IT IS INSIDE…"

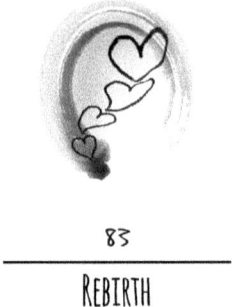

83

Rebirth

Rebirth is - like death - is infinitely natural. Rebirth happens all the time. Nothing remotely religious or spiritual about it. Nothing inorganic or mystical there if you understand it's just a part in nature.

You are literally reborn in consciousness each day. The person you get out of bed as in the morning has not got much to do with the person you have been "lately" or the person you'll become in the future. It is a vortex of possibility that dreams create as you unconsciously die and are returned again back to Earth with a new possibility ingrained in you, something new is always reborn in your sleep, there is a brand new opportunity and yes, a brand new or tweaked at least organism as much of you rejuvenates and regenerates itself. It is good to understand this. Each day is holy cycle. It has it's own ideas and creative opportunities like no other day like it. Each day the Earth turns to it's very special beat. You just levitate out of one state into the next without noticing it: always refreshed and rebirthed even though you might not feel so.

Cherish that. You are a hologram, a quantum being constantly reborn.

You have many choices.

"YOU ARE A HOLOGRAM, A QUANTUM BEING
CONSTANTLY REBORN.
YOU HAVE MANY CHOICES."

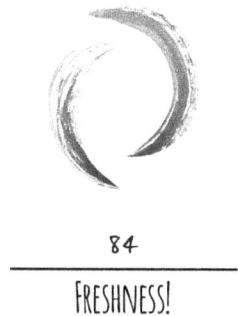

84
Freshness!

If you think you are not a fresh new version of yourself today - you're lying.

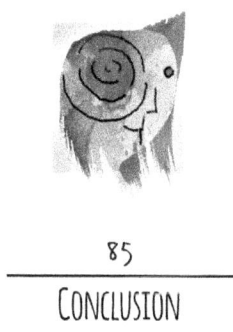

85
Conclusion

Time to count the chickens my dear.

Let's bring this sequence to a nice tight closure and create a much needed conclusion right here. In the last sequence of intensity, did you find yourself? Have you finally started walking towards you? Yes? Are you able to be happy yet? Yes?

Pull yourself out of this rut. Become it. Definitely no more reading. Start being!No?

Well, lets look into you and see what gives.

Hmmm…

Are you hungry? No?

Are you thirsty? No?

Are you tired? No?

Then what are you doing here on your butt, pondering? If you are bored, you aren't well. If nothing ignites – you need to go inwards. Explore! Nothing happens here, it is all inside you!

86
Growth

Are you grateful?

It would be so fine if you were for a while.

Yes, in deep serenity, introversion and grace there is room to sow a seed and become something even more! Are you though, able to do the gratitude thing? If you do not like your own company or don't have the attention span to glorify what is here for you in all simplicity - it's not easy to find the new Earth to plant your seed upon. It's hard to find the new version of tomorrow if gratitude is not creating joy.

Maybe in some solitude you'll find the seed you want to sow. There are plenty of opportunities for you, you just have to be grateful for what you already have. Otherwise it's hard to start new things. Prepare the soil of tomorrow by tending to the soil of today.

Go within. Relate back. Empty your pallet again and start from within.

Start it now.

Not shaking the old paradigms easy?

"...GRATEFUL..."

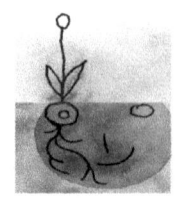

87
Perseverance

Still reading, still going huh? You poor thing. Let go. Not letting go? That's not too bad.

We have a hero here, don't we?

We have somebody who will get to the "top" "no matter what"!

There is a reason for that and yes, a dark one. Best of luck, but still, this isn't too bad.

If you cannot take what you need quickly, joyfully and run with it (like all animals are designed to do) - you might feel within that you're destined for "something better". A breakthrough, no, an evolution, a revolution even! And there is a feeling maybe that the longer you stick to it, the more it will give you!

Perseverance is an endless cycle of madness.

It makes it hard to see the bigger picture and embrace serendipitous opportunity that the universe is so willingly giving at all times. So let go, or if it is hard to let go - please go on reading. On and on and on and on. It's all just a dance with yourself anyway.

Are you perhaps somehow very well connected to it all? Do you feel you know pretty much everything? Are you secretly thinking;

"WE HAVE A HERO HERE, DON'T WE? :)"

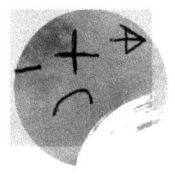

88
Primitiveness

"I am evolved, I am better than others, I protrude somehow, I am different. I am better than what I have in front of me. I am content. Me me me. It's all here – right here. I am the king/queen of evolution."

Are you there? Do you have a calcified pineal gland perhaps with a very strong image in your head of "exactly" who you are? Is there a little shiny halo sticking out from the back of your head on boastful days? You got wings yet? Do you consider yourself the better part of the day for someone? That's great. Please continue through this book. Read it over twice if you can.

If you do feel elevated and as if there's no more to know or see anymore almost - there needs to be a way out of this. It is nice to be within self and yes, selfishness is great too, but if you feel the centre of all things beyond other people's worlds completely – it is tired and limiting for you. Nothing happens there for a long time or if it does it is not savoured or truly explored and expanded through. Things get stuck, getting to the truth of things isn't easy either as most of it isn't found or tasted. The most boastful ones are often fools and yes have to work hard for all of us in a funny erroneous way. If self protrusion and levitation over this "simple world" is something you feel often - you have to find your feet. If you are constantly frowning at the world yet feel elevated beyond it, there is a real issue here. There is a boundary with creation.

If you do feel that you are "better than" what you are usually sometimes or that which you see, if your stature in this world is perceived through elevation over somebody or something in your life – that's good. Just keep thinking that for now. Maybe in some wondrous way you will create so much inward thought and feeling that it'll all fall down and collapse. It is possible.

Through too much self obsession and false optimism a new opportunity to burn it all down arises and yes, this part of you that feels awesome today will one day become some type of shame or burden as the tables do have to turn sometimes. If elevation is your game – chances are it will need to collapse for you to see the opposite very quickly or very strongly one day. It's a topsy-turvy little ride but it does come with a prise – abundance of opportunity to prove yourself wrong.

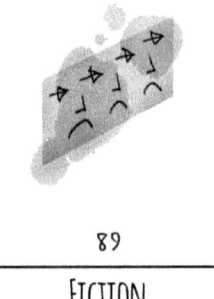

89
Fiction

You are fictional?

You are living an idealic fictional reality if you presume yourself as a character in a movie - the good, the bad, the ugly or any other more elaborate type cast for you. Do you feel it is important to fit to a mould or a special type of screen play for your life? It would be amazing to see that in action yes, whatever you feel is best to create – but would that serve you and your purpose? Quite likely not.

if you think of you as a piece of character development – a feasible tool to know more and feel better with every hurdle overcome or with each move played like a hero in a film – you are creating an unnecessary game plan which turns into unnecessary energetic outpours. This life becomes a sort of proper game of behaviour and thought – not the wild adventure that people want to experience. The wild ride of life is mistaken for a scene after scene melodrama which can't lead towards you only on the way to disaster.

This life is designed to be holy openness. It is meant to be uncandid and connected to as much opportunity as you can handle. A staged life is a splashy neurotic dance with the possibility of life, but not it's true potential. A fictional life is a road to insanity. Are you constantly asking: "Which mountain am I going to climb next?" as a sort of feat for the character you have created of yourself. Without reason else than "It'll look good on me". Then you possibly are here living a fictional life. What's wrong with this picture? We are told it is a good one, but what is here really?

Inability to be oneself.

Can you just be?

Just be there - with just you – content as just yourself? Just you in this room or you at this place... Can you feel reality shifting as you are still as stone? It is all loving you and is all obvious. You can't imagine being held just like that? A stable, self creating, self generating obvious easy and fulfilling reality? Lets try to get out of this pickle. Please read on

90
Perfection

Still but moving, full but empty.

Searching eternity over for that magical land of perfection?

Is it hard to get there to this holy sweet spot between sensations?

Between light and dark, fulfilment and hunger, real but spiritual, in love but free? Isn't it hard?

That's why you have here this book in front of you that you're still touching with your poor little hands that are sad from turning pages and your cute little eyes that are blinking sad blinks from watching little spots of ink change shape on the page you are reading…oh dear. Here you are.

A hero.

Quite often a hero feels nothing else is appropriate but perfection. That sweet little word. That funny little world of eternal search.

If you can't just be simple, if you can't quite feel it…the feeling of joy beyond this book right now - we have a winner, or rather, a person that can't win ever. In which there is truth as much as is lie.

A shaman at work. The searcher of the ultimate dream.

And that is truth. So be it.

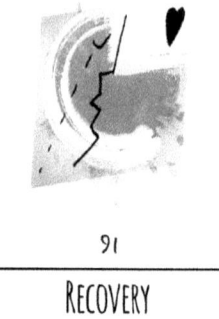

91
Recovery

Are you truly trying and trusting you will get there? Are you going and going and going, reading and reading, running and running, working and working, trying and trying? Are you?

Cool. That's your endlessness and that will never change till you can't: Can't read anymore. Can't write anymore. Can't run anymore. What are you burning yourself out for? Why do you have to fight life in order to progress? What is the need for strain here? Evolution? It won't take you far if you are stretching yourself too thin. You must allow time to process, relax and become.

Just as an athlete needs to still before the big performance, just as the hunter needs to lay into the grass before the timely pounce, just as the muscle tissue needs time to recover after the gym – we all need to recover energetically, psychically and emotionally. We otherwise stretch ourselves thin and have nowhere to be next. The road ends abruptly for those who do not know how to stop. Don't overdo it.

Release.

> "THE ROAD ENDS ABRUPTLY FOR THOSE WHO DON'T KNOW HOW TO STOP."

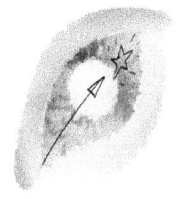

92
Determination

Do you want to do better next time? Do you want to be bigger and do bigger things?

Oh my friend, how wondrous is that! You want to evolve your craft, your culture, your expectation of yourself, your family line or your parent's expectations of you? Do you want to be the brick in the wall of your family that did better than the bricks before it? Do you want to be that brick or just the brick layer of your dream?

You are a brick. Suffice with that. How does that feel?

93
Servicing

Are you becoming another brick in the wall?

Pink Floyd. The Wall - great album. Good brick.

Perhaps you may not see it now, but you are just a brick in the wall. A great brick perhaps but still, a brick for it's own place in someone else's history or someone else's life - a brick laid down for even greater bricks and structures to come. If we are constantly thriving only for something or someone else, building ourselves up for "something" – we are just bricks in a way. Not much else. Self dedication to a service unless is part of a maturity initiation (that shouldn't take long) - is sad, disregarding and dangerous.

So tell yourself, as the brick you are becoming through service and pushing forward for someone or something else - do you want to keep going up and up and up this way, Building the Great Wall of China for nothing?

If service isn't enjoyable part of play – you are servicing for nothing.

If you have awakened and you do not want to be a brick in the wall, stop reading for now. Go for a walk, enjoy the Moon, the Sun. Find it in the simple life, not in the complexity of your journey. Just feel for now.

Is that hard? Are you clenching, still going? Feeling purposeless?

Please read on.

94

Status

Status is the creation of yourself into a powerful person offcourse - the brick of bricks! Becoming the best brick!

The big brick, the golden brick. The big special brick of cheese maybe. The biggest, most esteemed brick of cheese that has ever been! Aged, trialled, trusted, branded and put away onto a dusty shelf at a prestigious deli for very special ceremonial consumption in due time.

Perhaps one day this cheese will be devoured for a very special, prestigious occasion with a very special bottle of expensive French wine. Perhaps. It would be quite a feat – to be able to become an objectified version of your former self wouldn't it? Yes there is glory, there is also fear of not being in regard which is something left over from your upbringing, which must be as time goes by transcended. Deep need to be precious to someone isn't real. It is long lost emotional instability from childhood.

Would you like to come along, to mould with me a little? Want to keep pulling on that dream of status, abundance, the dream of ageing to perfection? Want to go to all the fancy cocktail parties with me and wear the special pants with me?

Let's go dear one. Let's shuffle onto the next sequence and maybe we might see the purpose of status in our culture together.

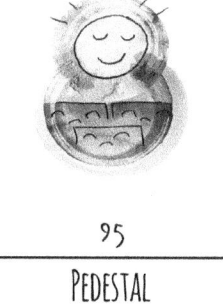

95
PEDESTAL

You are. Just are….you are you. Your own elevation and your own lull. The contrast is yours – all yours. But perhaps you want to accentuate your contrast with others. That is fine, let see what it brings.

If you're not just happy to be human yet, we understand. Let's spice things up. Perhaps a "specialty" for you is in order. Let's give you a title. Hmm, lets see. So you're not just a brick in the wall or on the cheese on the shelf…you are the wheel.

Pedestal makes you feel as if you are not at least something else. And that is very fine. You are The Wheel - Not a brick at least. It may mean more freedom. It may bring more confidence, but in the end you are still using yourself for something. By seeking pedestal you are descending into something very small – objectification by another person.

You don't have to be put away or put towards something that you "represent" or "thrive through". Yes, purpose might be a middle name of yours for now, but as a wheel, you must master yourself through your own special standards, which is exciting. You can be here today, there tomorrow in your fancy car with your fancy counterpart or without…. do you want to be that? The free person that looks to another as unbound or special somehow?

Why not just cut the bull and be it now? You are the "better" wheel of cheese that doesn't come in brick form anymore. Is that all there is to you? Maybe what you are is enough? Maybe you are enough always? Offcourse, if you want you can roll in your Ford Corolla around the coast for now and imagine what being the big expensive wheel of cheese in a Lamborghini is all about, but what about that do you want?

Perhaps for some it's not actually about the Big Cheesiness – the status or the position of power in front of other people. What if it is just about the fancy car and the lifestyle that matches?

Let's look into that (please go on reading my superficial friend)

96

PRIVILAGE

So, being the presentable, unique and very valued Big Cheese is not enough? You want to be the Alice in Wonderland or the Mad Hatter at your very special overflowing table with rabbits, mice and tea? That's a deep little rabbit hole!

Lets recap very quickly – you are born alone with nothing else. You have all you need inside you, but perhaps if you are here, there is no use telling you this. Maybe it's been lost – the concept of ultimate freedom through a few generations of your bloodline. That's ok. Lets get these DNA strands back to where they should be.

To understand privilege completely – just look at all objects of privilege. All the place keepers of privilege, all the systems and the symbols of it: the physical ones, the mental and spiritual ones too. What is behind need for privilege and power as an entity? Meet it.

Maybe look at how hard the people have to work on the other end to make these things come to life for very few. See what is the worth of that labour and how much time it steals from people's lives.

Greet your creative need for collection with respect for now if it doesn't touch your heart to know what it takes to create a privileged group set apart from the "others". Perhaps it is time to look it in the face and see the full chain of events it takes to get someone all the way up to great prestige and privilege at the top. It might not feel too bad - in that case you are here for the right reasons. If you feel no empathy for the chained up world that had to work so hard to generate this opportunity, you will have to understand it somehow. You too will one day be one of them on the other side - just to develop empathy again. Just to close the gap between that and this.

Have you got no concept of how strange the idea of privilege is? Perhaps not. Well, lets help your overgrown conditioning wake up out of the dream. If It helps, it may be nice to return to chapter 75 and read a bit on False Intention.

Lets read on.

97
Needs

Do you want it ALL?

The holidays, the get-aways, the swanky technology, the gadgets, the little clicks and the big ones, beautiful people, parties and soirees, ecstatic music, the works. Or at least some of that. You want something? You desire.

Offcourse needs can be different for different people, but despite their position in the world or how they are seen in society, needs are needs. They are a product of low self worth.

Do you want to come check it out in secret, or do you want greater fun and the ability to be at the top of that dream as the provider, the persecutor, the conductor, the grand master, the big boss, the Big Cheese, the whiskey and the champagne too? Oh wow. How….sad.

Wake up. You are not worthy in some way. Pease read on.

98
Inner Value

Are you not worthy right here, right now, just as you are?

Are you not worthy if you don't have what you think one of your kind should have? Do you have bigger things always on the mind? Can you not stop and feel prestige in just a breath of air or a drink of water? Why are you hiding parts of yourself in things that can not be attained or fully understood?

Do you feel unworthy? You are wrong. Lets break you out of this. Please read on.

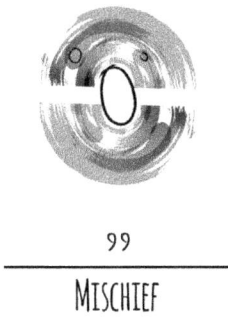

99
Mischief

Been a bad boy or girl?

Do you need to be punished? Do you want yourself as a sort of punching bag today, maybe a door mat tomorrow, the king himself and the king's squire the day after? Do you fluctuate between ability to be regal or grand and the need to be somehow seen as cunning or abused for something?

Do you want to serve and to please the big game players in order to be in your own little game better off? How appalling! Wake up. This is need for punishment. You might need to recognise perhaps that you are creating a story here that you yourself are in punishment of yourself for. Wake up. Your greater self wants much more from your journey than just this.

This was an interesting option of book for you then. You are in the right place here and too bad that you're not at ease enough to recognise peace – to stop reading now. Take this moment to laugh and put away your toys.

If you're playing sticky little games still and don't know how to stop, please go on then and think twice each time before you start something you do not care to experience. Fall into you not outward towards things that cannot fulfil.

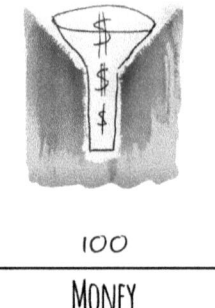

100
MONEY

Rich. You are. You are born rich. You have much that your body can provide always!

You have muscles to punch, you have eyes to see, you have ears to hear, you have legs to walk and so much more! Your body is a gold mine through which you connect to so much immeasurable wealth of this world, through which you burst unlimited energy enough to power a whole city! You have people to meet and places to see and so much unexplainable things waiting for you! Just by being alive - you are born wealthy. Not good enough?

Well, why not be rich? Financially so. Why not? Why not take over the world or at least a little corner of it? Why not have monetary power? Because it's stupid, that's why.

You could be though, you know that? It's true. And yes there is a giant Rabbit hole that goes with greed so let's have a look at that my little Alice in Wonderland. Please take my paw, lets go frolicking in the next bunch of thoughts if things are not still clear…why wealth of the financial type is still a beckoning to you? Perhaps this is why:

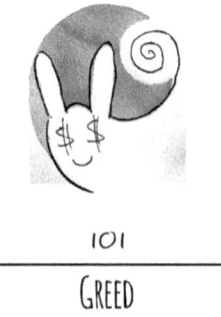

101
GREED

How far does the rabbit hole go? Rabbit hole, rabbit hole - how big are you?

This is not for monetary greed only, all greed. We experience it more than we expect. Through need of partnerships, need for commitment, need for gain, success, achievement, exploration – if we feel deeply and fully towards something beyond ourselves – we are in greed. We are in the rabbit hole.

Down the rabbit hole goes into the abyss and it don't return you back quickly. If you think you want it – whatever you elevate beyond this reality – if you really want it, it slowly becomes you and sometimes even slowly swallows you whole. Greed is like sinking sand. And yes, parts of you have been lost to many things perhaps already that you really wanted to achieve, to escape through, to create.

They don't come back easy – those missing pieces of you. That is why we have to change things a lot after relationships or we have to create greater expectations of ourselves after the ending of trips and other life changing events. We have to starve out of our patterns, to try hard to change something just to get ourselves back to our natural state if we have been sucked in by any kind of human greed. That is - if we want to regain what we have lost through what we thought was attainment.

The wanting gets bigger and bigger. It burns a great big gaping hole in your world that sucks in things and it doesn't return them back easily. Energy is lost, relationships suffer, time is bent and eventually health and true happiness can abandon you too.

If you feel you need the feeling of ambition and greed deeply, then you are lost in something beyond your own world, your own cause and your own feeling. You are gradually sucked in, and you become in ways greed itself – the being for suction of energy   though on the surface you might be seen as someone perfectly fine, perfectly good.

Sometimes yes, we are given and it seems easy. It doesn't own us. Cocaine doesn't own Madonna either. But in any case, to be weary of all elevation beyond other beings is wise as it can be very corrupting.

> "JUST BY BEING ALIVE –
> YOU ARE BORN WEALTHY"

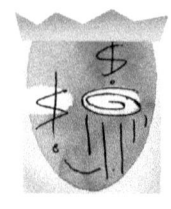

102
Manifestation

Wanting happy, wealthy, easy discoveries? I do, don't you? Yes! We all love an easy outcome!

Feeling and knowing that one day there is a pot at the end of the rainbow is a good feeling, isn't it. A big heavy pot filled with gold that makes dreams come true! We suppose that can benefit us ALL! (or so we suspect before the pot becomes clearly seen)

Don't fall for it: Easy gain. Easy discovery of something pretty and shiny. Stop that. Follow your own journey. All is delivered.

Leprechauns are sneaky creatures.

Ease and abundance knock on the door often, we just don't recognise it because it may not wear the pretty disguise of monetary wealth, otherworldly success or any other kind of fluffy elevation.

Sometimes the gifts of the universe are just a good friend or a nice feeling inside. A piece of bread at your mother's house. But, do you notice it when that wealth comes? Probably not. We want to MANIFEST something don't we here? Something BIG - that's the latest craze after all isn't it. Or at least, that is what they want you to feel. What ever better to work with then a bunch of "wizards" who want nothing more than easy spoils.

In consistently snooping out the effortless win or the fast gain, you are a fool for it all. The fool for that which seems "better" to you than that which is present and always, constantly given. Of course, this "better" is always easy to love, isn't it, but quite often what we have gets unbalanced and overwhelmed when we introduce a new scheme, a spectacle of easy creation that isn't actually in alignment in time or even in tune with our energy. So we do get sometimes what we tremble for, but it isn't easy. We loose a lot as well.

Put away all fantasies that tell you to manifest whatever you want whenever you want – as often the greed that budges us towards that kind of thing isn't clear on us – it doesn't know who we are and what we have got is precious. It wants something there for it is not clean. And in that is a sort of envy of the past or a neediness for the future. Without this feeling we all can do.

The feeling of easy growth and fast gain is indeed the latest craze considering – it is contagious and the crazy need for easy manifestation has made much money for itself as a prophecy of sorts since the early 60's and exploded again in early 2000's. All aboard the quantum train! Everybody comes! Remember when they said the same thing before the industrial revolution destroyed our eco systems? Perhaps you will understand why this is similar.

When we accomplish very little inside but we learn to pull on the strings that make things "come" – we devolve. We result in nothing unless we truly pray or hope for something that is in alignment with our source journey. It would be nice to know that first before you understand what abundance is, then when you recognise you already have it – open for more, but not until you are ready through acceptance of what you are already with. The ability to manifest is indeed blinding but it is in a way also perfectly created just so – as we who do not play with greed create more in our own journey line then usually would be available – while the world is obsessed with things that do not make anyone or anything happier.

The fun part is that the leprechaun you are becoming in the process of ease-chasing is blessed with friendship always, ironically. People do love the promise of a shortcut and if you do vibrate it as a given strategy, the likeliness of people coming to greet you is high. We do not want you for you, we just want to taste that amazing flavour of intense greed turned rainbow. However, this gift is not real. Neither are the friendships often, which to much surprise tend to sting a bit in the end.

Keep 'em coming, the army of treasure hunters! All together now! Trick or treat!

> "FOLLOW YOUR OWN JOURNEY
> ALL IS DELIVERED."

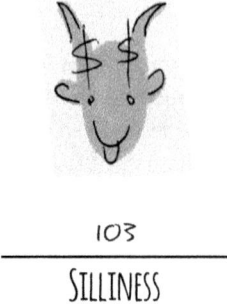

103
Silliness

Silliness and uncoordinated impulse.

You are becoming a funny little Leprechaun if you are wanting yourself to thrive above other people. If you aim high you might achieve, but when will you learn to be elegant and graceful? When will you accept and realign with peace?

Neverrr!

So lets read a little bit more

You are becoming too small for your purpose if you are after gain and elevation, which means that the show is over for us and often we are not enticed by you beyond the first glance. The charismatic person is always on the stretch towards themselves. The non charismatic person is tired of themselves, they are reliant on their demeanour. That is why neediness and deep nagging wound of never being tall enough above others becomes disfigurement in later years. It may not seem true – but we are not trying to touch your statements. We do not care to achieve over each other. We just want to be free.

If you are looking to heave yourself towards some form of "big success" through this type of books, looking for the best ideas to get yourself upwards, hungry for more shortcuts - the point has been lost. Intensity is not creative when one wants to expand. Energy of loss and depletion is more likely to help with elevation if you are constantly trying for something. By reaching upwards you are small. When you recall that all is just beautiful – you release and a vastness takes over. More opportunities come through breath and openness than through tightness of your spirit.

There was definitely gold in this book in the first two thoughts I have to say. Maybe three. That was all the wisdom you needed. That was the little pot of gold right there. Maybe you can understand why if you read those again.

Now we're just digging in the depth of the human psyche together - making this book into a possibility of profitable sale on my end, and you my little searcher of wonder and delight are stuck in a pot of gold that doesn't need to be.

Yet you are perhaps ready to make the change which is the worthiest part of being silly once upon a time.

Please read on. You might as well.

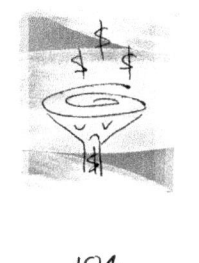

104

Captivity

Oh no! Our little leprechaun is stuck in a pot of gold!

You're a little leprechaun me laddie, how ever are you going to get unleashed into life again without more riddles of illusionary success? Just as you are – free and hopefully open for changes and games without cruelty.

Start walking around, use your feet. If you are stuck your feet are likely to be sticky too! See what people need and how you can help maybe. What is it that people live through? What is their story and how is it true for them? Find yourself through your speech and the possibility of connection with another within which you find a new identity for your life. Find your way here through the simple things that are around. You might not be so stuck at all!

Great power (even for someone a little greedy) comes with great responsibility, so if you are wondering how I can justify or explain my lifetime to me - start spending up large and don't think of it, as it is better to be a leprechaun searching with the soul of a lion, than a wallet with no personality. It's not important if you don't succeed this time. It never is. Just loosen up and the more opportune strategy will create itself!

"...LOOSEN UP..."

105
MATERIALISM

A walking wallet with no brain, personality or heart. Is that where you are going?

Are you someone who is wealthy yet spends on themselves alone without helping anyone else? Maybe you might feel that they don't care about you - which in time becomes true. They do not and never would at this point maybe, even if you bought them the world.

Have you got paradise in mind? Want to go there alone?

But what would I do there alone?

Are people becoming 2D cut outs? Are they so far away from you because you're too wealthy, sexy, prosperous or intriguing? Can you no longer identify other people's worth?

Best pay "someone" to be there or at least entertain you right?

Dehumanisation and spoilt relationship with money and power go hand in hand my dear wallet, which leaves you with very little really. Just a cardboard experience for you to chew over.

There you are. Your wallet self is happily entertained when an option is created through wealth and performance until another wave of self pity comes. Intrigue yourself with something rather than your worth. You might find it fascinating.

Perceive life (artificially at first maybe) in a freeing, serendipitous way. It will hold hands with you and you will feel united again. Promise. You can!

"YOU ARE BORN FREE"

106
Expenses

If your happiness costs money, you aren't just stuck, you're paralysed.

Does it cost you to laugh better or to eat better than other people? Does it cost you to be seen where you are seen or to do what you like to do? Would it cost you to start up that company or get that great story going? Is it coming down to the dollar today? Is that all it takes to be who you are going to be yet you aren't making any steps?

If money isn't here, it's not here for a purpose. You don't need it. Your reality doesn't support it. If it's not available, that's great – there are other ways to grow, and often there are bigger ways to explore! Start thinking big. Not practically – emotionally. Awaken your senses. Create more freedom and more room to breathe through your circumstance. More feeling. More pride!

If you still think you need money, you're a little stuck here.

You might have a habit.

"A HABIT IS DESIRE TO MAKE THINGS END."

107
Habits

The habit that you wear. Does it make you a priest or a rabbi? Maybe a monk. Maybe something a little less intentional. A habit is a way of life and in it is your curse and cure at the same time for your whole lifetime. A habit shows you what you need inside not on the outside. It welcomes in change, but can you see it?

Your habit. Everyone has at least one. Does it make you feel special? Does it supply you with a special feeling that you could only generate with that thing, space, time or person? It's ok, we've all been there for some reason. It's not good but it is welcome by this society grid though on multiple levels of people's lives and experiences. We understand you better sometimes through the habit alone than through your deeds and thoughts.

If you are in a habit of something, you have something within you that is insufficient. It is more than it seems on the outside. There is a thing you do wrong or that you think wrong – you are in partnership with something beyond you perhaps through the external thing or even a way of life that the habit provides. It's a closure, a habit is desire to make things end.

It's not scary or bad no matter what you do – if you work too hard or if you take heroin, there is no difference – those are both serious habits. The main purpose of them is to escape. To leave a full stop somewhere where it usually cannot be. To create a new frontier perhaps out of that stop. The morning coffee is that. Your cigarettes are that too. What are you trying to end? Think of that not the habit.

Are you uniformed somehow here? Do you owe somebody or something the money the time or the thought that you generate through this cyclical experience? In the feeling of debt is where all habits come from. The guilt makes the habits possible and also makes them part of the daily cycle of discontent. Know that you have no debt here to begin with. You are born free.

Perhaps one day when you are enraged by your actions you will no longer support your habits as they are often the ones to fall out of great big rage against self for creating some form of trap, a very stilling experience here. A habit is a subduing factor to your life and yes, the clipping of wings to your freedom.

You're not a slave. If you think you can't escape you might like being one, please read on...

108
Dependency

So, you're slaving away. You are captivated or captive. You are barely surviving on some plane of this experience, as that energy of bare survival makes the Ophelia story complete. The cycle closes and there seems to be just no way.

That is the best way to get stuck and yes, smothered over and subdued. It does create a sort of "life of peace" encompassing the ideal of fait as the main component so no injustice is seen. Karma – the way they preach it today – is the perfect example of self deceit and internal need for smothering, for being ridden, for being pushed, for being smothered and smoothed over into something formless. Into something not very much. That is not peace. It is a false story dreamt up for you – a life of lie that is unfolding over and over again. The life of captivity. And there are so many spiritual and cultural constructs to support that too. Beware of false submission into something out of faith. There is a trickster at play.

Born free. You are. That is all.

In the captive's dream, you are supporting your habit which in turn makes you feel that you are supported by it. A deed, an income source, a person, a condition – something is pushing you onwards into the depth where you do not belong. But, you must like it for some reason if you do not want to be free. And no it is not weakness and it is not fear. It is you.

Some captivity cycles can become whole lifestyles, yet often they go misunderstood and misinterpreted. This is worse as you do not recognise the loop that is coming to complete full circle - which in the end becomes a very strong pattern or even an eternal part of you for lifetimes.

When you are completed by your own slavery as a loop of life - it becomes beyond slavery – here you count yourself one with your master. One with void that makes you persevere in a direction or a way of life that has nothing to do with you. Wake up! You are not born captive. There is no suffering on this planet that is not self inflicted. Release and choose peace.

If you do not think it is possible to be happy here and you think that you have to sell or slave yourself, to become something over and over for some obscure cause, "god" or purpose – you need to wake up. To recognise that you are playing with yourself a cruel and awful game. There is no "power" that is pushing you anywhere. It is you – it always has been you. And it is you that has to answer to you for it.

You have to make it out of this loop and it has to be now.

Are you that submissive particle in your own world that you are yourself creating? Think again! Can you riddle yourself out of you yet? No? Lets keep going then. Please keep reading.

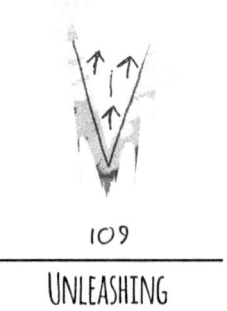

109

UNLEASHING

What is it that is behind this inability to be at 100%?

Let's see – if you are still reading then perhaps you are still stuck.

Do you think you need habits keep you going? Habitual lifestyles, choices, people, circumstances, money? Do you still think you cannot feel or live for free? Despite most pages of this book reminding you that you are enough, do you still not feel the shift?

You are humorous! But some good hard work must be done. And it won't be unfun.

Do you still think you can't just walk and function as you are designed in unison with yourself? Do you still think you can't allow yourself to speak your truth through music or word? Is there lack of faith? Do you have to call text or just watch people be something instead of express and radiate? Wow. We are stuck! There needs to be a creative unleashing here to help you start yourself up again!

Understanding of the captive state of your mind already creates an opportunity for a freedom. Just understanding how far you have gone and what you have received as you wake up to your senses creates a great catalyst for change and for greater union with truth. It would be so nice to see people wake up and yes – become wild again. Awaken to the feeling of what everything has become over time. Awaken, connect the dots - to see the bigger scheme of life love and care available at all times. No regrets eventually only the new acceptance of life. It would be an amazing experience to watch the world unleashed one person at a time.

Let's start with you.

110

Beastliness

The beast? "The" beast!

You have to be that sometimes. You have to! And it isn't bad or good. It's natural.

Becoming beastly in yourself is not right or wrong, religious or non religious, spiritual non spiritual or any type of contrast to the oneness that is all things…it's just the ability to vibrate at the optimum level, combining both light and dark to connect to greater blueprints of reality. It is the big bang. You are the big bang, and yet most people feel uncomfortable knowing that.

We are afraid of it, and so this energy is untameable. This natural vibration is wild and very dangerous when feared indeed. It becomes the energy that makes wars happen, it is the energy of death and life holding each other by a thread – a destructive force that feels unnatural and evil. However, this great force is always welcome should it be not feared.

Without fear beastliness in itself is faith for bigger brighter things and the conclusion to ideals that aren't any longer sufficing.

If your own thought and inspiration is not doing you any good, the beast has to awaken. Destruction and creation in one must take form. This energy is beyond words or instinct. It is the raw truth of you. The shadow that everyone hates and the light that is too bright to see!

"YOU ARE THE BIG BANG."

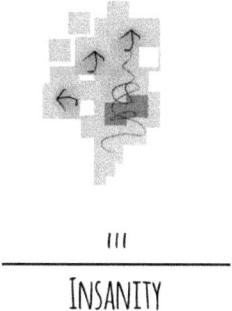

III
INSANITY

To become the beast – the mad creator - is to be a little bit on the insane side at least. To truly give it your all – to dissolve your whole experience into that one thing or moment – to become absolute. This concentrated outpour is what brings great light.

Although here is the blade of shadow too. All great creators: underbelly dwellers, criminals, poets, giants, mathematicians, eccentrics and other exceptional people have done this. They have used their shadow and the overpowering need to design brand new concepts.

The fluctuation between shadow and light creates insanity and it is what makes the biggest creations possible. It is not sad or volatile, it is focused and amused by the phenomenon of alchemy that takes place between shadow and light. It is an insane need to feel and to finally emit oneself in true form – with no exception and no restriction! It is crazy to encompass it – to contain it or to create through it – but it is the sanity's edge that is needed for ground breaking elevation and yes – reform.

Through insanity we create worlds that have never before been!

"THROUGH INSANITY WE CREATE WORLDS THAT HAVE NEVER BEEN."

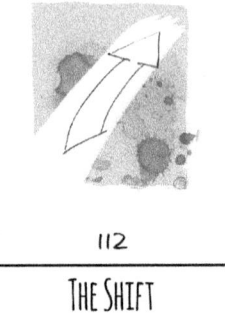

112

The Shift

You- the paradox, you – the shift.

The shift within is the mad force that connects to all things at once. Being this isn't easy, it is hard.

It's very terrifying actually, because we think we are not good enough, we think that we are nothing or that we are not allowed. There are so many natural laws that hear us shift and stand in our way. There are many people and beings that will not any longer be around us if we shift – so here we have a choice. To win we must release.

In being the shift or the shifter the stakes are high but in this paradigm all is possible and completely united.

We cannot roar yet for the most part – that is the power of the beast– only smile politely and say nice things sometimes because we are cursed with the desire to fit in over the deep need to connect. Sometimes making oneself a free person is hard – very hard and it's not the outside world that is holding us back. It is us. The ones who fear that we will no longer be ourselves after we acquire what we actually are born to acquire again in the current state of this planet– optimum freedom.

We spiral out of what we are for that reason to commit to greater change. We connect to alcohol and drugs because we want it so badly – to experience freedom and to be the shift. We sacrifice many lives for this shift on this planet and all because we do not believe it is possible to just stand up, to be ourselves and to make it happen as us – the natural human beings.

Therefor we run away from the shift while trying to capture it. But we have to trust – each one of us –

You are the shift. You are it.

113

Unconsciousness

We become unconscious when we are scared of the result of the moment. It's not bad. It is the energy of change that takes us out of ourselves out of fear. But sometimes you just have to be "that person".

Yes, the maniac. The embarrassing friend. The grotesque individual. The person who blasts shadow and light simultaneously as they try to conceive something new through rebirth and destruction. This life feels short, abbreviated. It feels like it has not begun just yet - as if time or any part of this reality just isn't a friend. The world is against me! It just isn't fair!

Embrace the person you become during unconscious emotional patterns. It is the shift trying to create itself into union. It is a part of you that's trying to find a way to fit with your heart and your soul again. Sometimes all it needs is to be embraced by the person who is creating it.

Intense unconscious behaviour is here for a reason. It breaks through a barrier that the person cannot stay focused for as it is too big a leap. It is not bad to be unconscious – some people are for a good reason. Do not judge these behaviours in others or yourself. Unconscious behaviour is fear of the brewing shift. It is the break up old patterns to be able to form into something better. There is wisdom in unconscious realities.

Being here let alone creating shifts is terrifying and strange. We understand – all of us do that on some level we have to play the game if we are here – the game of loss and joy - the painful game of happiness and disappointment…..so what is it – this thing? What is this feeling? Why can we not express it or let other people see it in us? What is this shame we feel against this amazing force of life and the nature of being human? We have a lot of depth to conquer and we feel it within us. It is helpless we feel, but all we need to do is ask.

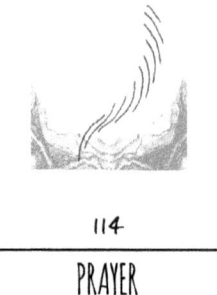

114
PRAYER

True prayer is a blast beyond all reason! This is the inertia times a million not a collection of spells. It is on the edge of itself – it is fearless openness to the opportunity to finally say what has been hidden. There is no power in ritualistic or formal states of prayer, neither is there power in bland states of life without feeling. Power that you need has to come from the heart. It is a roar and an upheave of your previous circumstance within the very moment of uttering.

Prayer is a deep cry for help.

It is a timeless inertia, the innocence behind separation.

It comes in many forms. Prayer takes place every day: it's in the way you look at life, the way you follow through each motion, however you do in your daily cycles – your life does involve prayer on the daily. It is in the fluctuation of your intensity as you choose every step of your life:

As you sit in traffic, as you look for your keys, as you wish for the phone to ring, as you worry about your parking ticket to still be valid, when you go to the store and you need something to be on the shelf– small things, big things - All these impulses and more are prayers. Believe in them.

Each part of you day that triggers you, that upheaves – listen to it – there is a truth in it and a part that is ready to be resolved – a prayer that is ready to be answered.

Wether your inertia is targeting the positive or the negative it doesn't matter – the focus and the intention both conscious or unconscious is a form of prayer. All creation is for success and abundance regardless of your energy outpour. All entwines and makes itself useful. No prayer goes unused, no energy push uncredited. All is economical in this universe.

You might have to allow yourself be completely seen – to become loose and obvious one day. To pray in a way of a profit, to always feel on the edge and off it too. That is not the path of weakness – it is a path of balance. That leads to a life of dream states and peaceful regularity of prayer. It is co dependant sometimes and accentuates itself forward through allowing sometimes other people to make choices for you as a part of a completely serene, co-dependent universe.

Or you might just have to bottle up sometimes and explode in creative ways instead – that leads to ups and down of deep penetrating times of prayer vortexes. You might have to be that strange person in the room, that eccentric maniac or that stupid person who cares – you are praying for the world. If you are bursting at the seems with something - within that is an important focus – you are praying for us, you are doing it for all creation. Understand your power, use it wisely.

Prayer is the use of universal energy that surges towards greater stories.

Prayer is using your own inner voice to shout you through space and time.

All is energy, it's all sound. You are just the prayer of yourself as you go on your way anyway, but not only a prayer of yourself. The prayer of all creation that wanted you on board.

Through great intensity, inter-dimensional shifts of great purpose are achieved. As you use yourself sparingly think about that – what would it give me to live this way? Sadly, tiredly, calmly? Would great outburst put my life into a different spectrum? Yes it would. And it would never change a thing at the same time. Your world would still be serene if that is what you discovered once upon a time. It is not about prayer as violence, it is not about forced intensity for greater shift. It's basically in a reminder that to go forward there must be splash.

Imagine as you sitting in a canoe, to expect the current to take you forward itself. It would do that eventually as that is how mind creates life. But, through intention and feeling of fury perhaps translated as a call for help, you row and through the rowing practice you connect together with greater consciousness, with your own heart and the need for more. That canoe is not just you – it is all things. You are dictating a life of love and care yes, but through grabbing the oar and paddling you are mending the trajectory into something of your own beauty, your own design.

"PRAYER IS USING YOUR OWN INNER VOICE TO SHOUT YOURSELF THROUGH SPACE AND TIME."

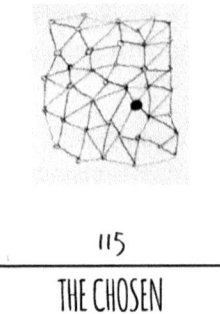

115
THE CHOSEN

We are all constantly chosen. A lot of us have no idea but we are often pushed towards action that isn't just uniquely homed within. Sometimes action is the reflection of all universe, the greater co creation.

This life is not just for you, though it is. It is connected to all of us. We all feel shame, we all feel disregarded and we all can't say a thing sometimes. Afraid to state, to ask, to understand. At times there's got to be a blast, and you my friend if you are feeling it, if you are on the edge of yourself have to generate it into physicality. If there is an intensity within and a depth to your internal vortex - you have been chosen to.

If you feel it - be it, blast it out, don't hold back. You are activated for a reason. Danger is only when we create a space for these feelings to be secret and silent. Bust out what you think, what you feel and what you have in mind if it is purging upwards. Become it. Impulse will run clear into greater work and mastery with time.

The feeling has to be stated outwardly, it must be transformed and passed on to the greater light, where it can be transformed into something of benefit. Inside it cannot dwell. It is no shame to feel pain or to act in violence that has been pent up for hundreds of years by you and the collective experience. We all feel it too. State it out - do not hide. Show us your true self. Be the call – the roar of the beast. The ancient cry for help. The summoning of creation.

Being one with us all in the state of prayer is a shamanic state: it is powerless and also very small. It is all itself needs to be. Intensity and what feels frightening has got much place in this world. It is welcome, all sound and light is welcome. All is one.

If there is a passion that is ripping you apart beyond this lifetime, beyond all things and it's making you feel so much intensity that is ongoing, this isn't bad. It might not happen straight away, but the energy has to be placed in the face of you at least, the creator and other people. Expose your feelings and tremble with delight.

Your personal evolution depends on it. Your personal evolution is a revolutionary one. For all of us.

116
Revolution

You the revolution.

The revolution is in you, not on the outside. If there is an emotional, neurotic process always taking place as if you are guided by something or somebody unseen towards greater knowledge and best creation - you can interpret this through great understanding of this world and pour it into craft, your daily means of conduct or even just physically through yourself.

Cherish this feeling of ecstatic worry or deep need. If you have something like that beating inside of you – there is passion and love and leadership that are growing where once was something painful or surrendered. The energetic intensity of this process as we alchemise our greatest shadow into light is freedom. It is never easy – it always hurts – as if you are just starting to come out of your ancient cacoon. Be the strong one here. Become who you were made to become. Caterpillar to a butterfly – it is destined.

This is a hard topic to see in the end….when you are realising that you aren't just you – the self – one limited identity spectrum – just one person. You are indeed the universe. The will of the collective mind. It is hard to see this and remain separate and own as you awaken to this. It is walking the line between sin and purity, between lust and death. It is a borderline state where you have to be the dream as well as the dreamer and yet, understand that what comes through you is not you entirely – it is the will of the collective mind.

It always has been so.

You are the insane, if you are here, if you have broken free too much unity of you to be able to go back to a single minded perspective, welcome. Let's read on.

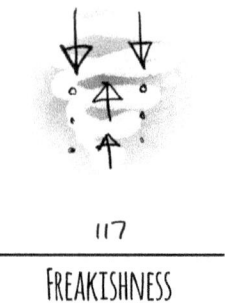

117
Freakishness

Perhaps you aren't a calm subdued evolution of your species? Do you burst and shift all the time? Do you run and hide inside just to find greater meaning over and over and over? You are not real to most people, because you aren't real somehow and it's not easy at this point to return or to step back in line anymore. The deed is done – you are over the threshold of security – you are a freak. You do not continue quests as prescribed - you have somehow been elected to be the revolution for us all in a totally different way.

You are a revolution under one skin if nothing seems right no matter how mindful and caring you are about the world that exists as it is. Should you be somebody who is living a prescribed human existence? Probably, but you cannot.

It is fantastic and scary at the same time when you understand there's no going back. You are a soldier. Perhaps you are not yet put together onto a new prism of yourself just yet. Perhaps you're still searching for some boundaries, something to keep you grounded and together with others. That's fine. We have that happen at least once, all of us.

We are all definitely designed to shift the status quo. If it takes us a lifetime that is good, for many it's a few.

You must develop clarity as a definite, just to be able to balance out the intensity you are choosing in your world if you do decide to go through this shift. Get down to the basics, wipe all things that aren't important. Start thinking clearly, start making things very simple for you. Start doing, creating, thinking differently and yes putting it into music, art, structure, whatever you feel will resonate best with your ascension codes. We are all designed genius, we all have an opportunity to shine. That is a way forward through history. Marvellous, if that is you – stop reading and start making. Start creating. Start doing. You're not just a freak – you are a poet that is able to change the world.

All energy is just that. It doesn't have to be perfect straight away how you channel that intensity. You can just start and the road will become lit as you go.

However, even though you understand that that is a feasible option – to become the first of your kind creator is on the cards. However, this might not come together for you if you are still worried about something in your world not coming together because of "you" – the new you that is coming through. Are you still feeling like the sore thumb that can't heal no matter what you do?

Don't be afraid of you - the monster. Please read on.

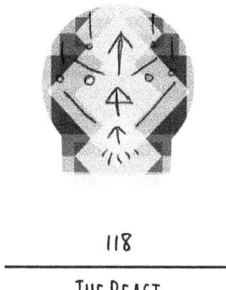

118

The Beast

You the monster, you the beast.

That which turns worlds, that which is constantly uncomfortable without avail. You are here? Are you still reading wanting to find ways for you forward out of this strangeness that is never subdued, always turning with no avail? Is there no way to find something to alleviate this energy? No release? You made it to this part of the book and in a way you made it….you have.

So you or parts of you understand the silliness of it all. The strangeness of creation. The badness of your life maybe or the badness that you are. Things aren't good. They just aren't. No matter what you do with it – your talent or your form. It just feels incomplete. That is actually good.

Lets have a look why.

You've got something in you that is remorseful only for the fact that you "are" and that is not easy to admit for us. Through this prism of your expression, all people and creation looks like surprise anecdotes of reality. Here we see a person who can't quite understand their purpose or the good that they are no matter what choices available, but they are breaking themselves trying. Over and over. Tears and joy in one. Constant pull of depth and light. What is that feeling? What is that space of being?

Death.

119
TRANSFORMATION

Death of that which once was "just you"- birth of that which is for All creation.

Death is never final. It is constant. We are ascending as we live our lives, so the old has to husk away. In order to live great lives, a part of us must die. Just as when you were a baby you weren't going to be that forever. You became someone in all ways different in seven years, and then as you reached your teenage years you were somebody completely different again. That toddler or that teenager perhaps no longer exist but what has created itself out of those forms is now an elaborate being that creates it's own experience and moulds it's own life.

What is ascension? Grandness is not achieved maybe here through what we thought we may have designed ourselves before, but parts die until we cannot fathom who we are. That's the point – the old grid comes undone and folds away as we become something unconditionally evolved and nurtured by totally different things.

Transformation is a must. It is the point of our birth.

The more we are genuinely unrecognisable to ourselves in a big scheme of things, the more we disassociate from our previous consciousness grid, we associate instead with a deeper meaning beyond just "this is me". In time, through conclusion and delusion we become open to shed our shell completely – the constraints of a human lifetime, the ego and other conditions, which takes it's turn over and over. The process of self rebirth never stops. In the end it does bring something before unexperienced – great consciousness explosions and greater deeper energetic lulls too. Each silent is stiller, each action is deeper. All makes itself larger and smaller. Things shift and yes in that passage is a potential for super human exploration of reality for sure. I hope this passage has created shift.

You are here.

Can you say to yourself – "Oh yeah, all is obviously perfectly self shedding and self creating" – can you see that ease of life and death? Can you play now? Can you just sense and feel? Can you just feel the energy here and become a free player in the game of life? Can you see it's simple?

No?

If not, you are just bashing yourself into you consciously, trying so hard to evolve or to result in something different perhaps. You are shifting and shifting and shifting yet there is never enough? Are you here? Is it never enough?

Read on. You're coming with me!

120

Power

Practice Tantra. Practice breath work. Practice energy harvesting and processing techniques. Get to yourself through yoga, through fitness or any other form of matter mastery. Stop thinking, stop following any story or use your time here for anyone else who doesn't need your input. Flow with the youniverse.

Circulate your energy inside, not on the outside. Become All.

Quit asking questions. You are the question and the answer to all your needs and desires. No partners. No parents. No gurus. No one to ask anymore. If you understand that and you are letting yourself stagnate through the question and answer entrapment through conversation with something or someone outside of you, that is great. Start walking – let everything go and be your own experience that understands itself through itself. Circulate your own power within yourself.

Lets begin. Ok so you are here, with me. You want to end something? Great. Do you want to start something up? Better. Circulate your energy inside and be the answer and the intention that burns in a nice flow inside. Imagine yourself as a hearth. The fire is your power. Let that energy in your heart guide you towards who you need to become, not me. Be that energy and the answer for you. Just one step in front of the other. Might start very obvious but it does lead you towards the greater purpose. The energy of your heart if you are thoroughly engaged with it, if you constantly follow through in depth and sincerity – it will lead you to what you need and you will last as a very deep impact in this world.

Slow, well formed, controlled, steady flow. All within. Breathe through it.

Power.

However, if you want to end things over and over beyond their value and start things again and again beyond their value too? Is there a compulsion here like a run away train maybe? Are you insatiable? That's not power, it's an avalanche.

Power without sensitivity as great as it may be is fleeting.

This creates ageing. This creates disease. This connects to cycles of depletion and sorrow even though the youthful days have had so much power and brawn in them. Power has to be developed over time, understood and cultivated.

You're not ready for the big change in you if there is an informal or frivolous energy within which likes to burst bubbles or punch in different directions thoughtlessly. If you are walking up to things and people (in your mind at least) needing them to be something more or less without care or energy of deep surrender – you have to learn how to circulate your power within you alone, not on the outside. Learn how to push and pull on this intensity in ways that don't disturb anyone else's peace. As you learn to push and pull in on what you are inside – you become alone and in that silence - all one

Power is a solidifying energy. It burns up fast when scattered, but yes, when harnessed inside – with great power comes great responsibility. It does connect to this world oddly or awkwardly when exercised. It must deeply imbed itself in something. To be a force, a brick, a rock. Something that isn't easy to shift or change perhaps. But also very light as you must learn to laugh at power when it comes. Power is like a pet dragon. Learn about it, play with it too but be wary it can strangle you too.

Who is that type of person who becomes such powerful presence they are otherworldly? Who is that person who becomes self enlightening always doing their own magical thing?

This isn't just power, it's mutation.

> *"YOU ARE THE QUESTION AND THE ANSWER TO ALL YOUR NEEDS AND DESIRES."*

121
Mutation

Mutations are mutiny inside one's own original blueprint given by nature. Have you been mutated by your trial and error personality? Have you tried to go for something that wasn't energetically compatible with you for a long time? Have you become someone completely unrecognisable from your family? You have betrayed your origins.

Why do we do this? Why make life so difficult?

If you are there maybe you don't think you're human anymore. Maybe you don't want to be. That's why we do it. To create a brand new type of timeline.

Your senses and your mind might be on edge often if you are transforming. It's not easy or hard but does disassociate potentially. You may feel sore and in pain from every gulp of air you breathe, from each sight that you see as you step out into the world of people's wishes made real. You might feel sad in each thought and action that you experience in order to understanding the futility of it all.

Through that depth, something new arises. The fearless need to be an improved version of what is potentially possible now, and through that a new voice of God.

This is not self hate this is just a feeling of being the shadow outcome of what you have been destined to be. Ashamed but happy, content but angry. What is that feeling?

Shame for nature, shame of self, shame of this world.

.....

"BECOME ALL."

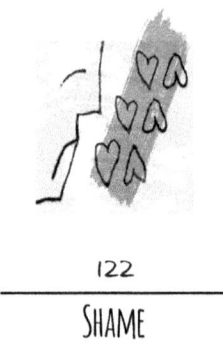

122
SHAME

What you are witnessing in this world is not shame – it is the natural flow of creation as it has created itself through this voyage. This intense world however polluted or strange – it is not a shame. It is sadness maybe manifested, but it is not a shame. It is a mature expression of source.

We have a polarity in us thinking that we have done wrong, that mistakes have been made and so we reflect badly on you and me. But we are not in the wrong. There are no mistakes only formulas. We are mathematically designed and so with mistakes they are possible because they are also manifestations of mathematics. Nothing more. We are exploring as we know how or as we knew how. It's not shame and shame shouldn't be.

But we have created it.

Shame is installed in us through deep nurture and un-combinable unity with what we feel is motherly or fatherly – dependency on something other than ourselves creates this within us. It's not true as a feeling. It is inconsistency of age. There is no true need for it but through perhaps hierarchical energy we have grown into…"children tired of being mistakes."

If you are here on this planet no matter what your parents have said – you are no mistake.

You are a perfectly fine and grand mathematical probability that is happy and welcome anywhere where it appears. You are designed to be here and yes, too make "mistakes".

Are you in shame for being here? The freedom thinker, the backward and forward player of the game of life, the sceptic, the self efficient portal, the thrust and the mellow, the sun and the storm? Are you afraid?

Don't be afraid.

You are pushed through life by many energies. You don't have to do anything you don't have to do. What you do has to change perhaps, yes, but you are not shameful.

It's just a matter of growing out of need to be embarrassed or a concern.

Be still.

You are grown, you are welcome, you have sovereign rights in this world, you are accepted by all creation.

You may not feel well enough within yourself about being here, that is fine and in ways becoming norm on this planet. You have to start feeling well within you. Become adult and open to accept greater life. In becoming free of societal upbringing you can create anything in your world. You just have to want it to happen. Pray - it will become clear. There is much possibility for so many quantum leaps. Just understand that it's ok to be sad or disappointed with it all sometimes. It's a fertile ground for a new beginning.

If you can't relate and all is painful in this world, you're lost. We can help you.

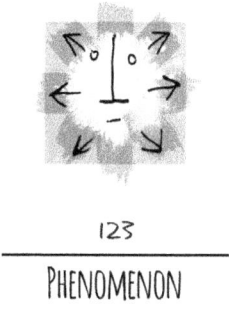

123

Phenomenon

Are you becoming beastly to yourself? The success and the failure all in one?

Are you a giant mind with so little to give or so little to live for still?

Would you consider yourself your family's shame yet a great success above them?

Think again. You are lost…

Even though your ego might confirm the opposite.

Place yourself into the negative spectrum here. "I hate it all" spectrum. It's ok, you know you are brilliant perhaps though you do not want to be it. You may know your special power though you feel "what is the use?" It is not uncommon. You are phenomenal. Too phenomenal for this reality maybe. Here is a shame and a power play in mind. There is more than enough hierarchical programming. We need to get you clear.

Please release through knowing….

No one understands the world if they feel they have finished the game.

Nobody.

Nothing is left to chance. The world is playing with you. Smiling

And if you think you know a thing or two about it beyond it….you have nothing.

You have nothing to do here? It's a trick.

Fight this feeling. Maybe that special friend that sits in your mind above the world and everything in it isn't a friend. It's a trap that leads right back to square one.

Let's find which way to now through the next sequence.

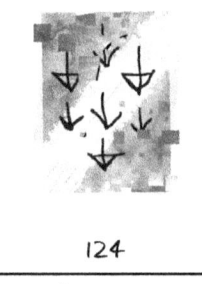

124

Sabotage

Self sabotage.

It comes in many disguises, flavours and varieties. I have known many as most creative individuals have perhaps experienced. Sabotage of self has a funky look and a confident smile sometimes and can be described as perfect or unique – it isn't. It is not hopeful. It's just un grounding.

There is no peace or freedom in being .nobody. in the end "by choice".

Being lost or admitting loss is fine. Sometimes loss is deeply self inflicted as one jeopardises their own life in order to feel "something". That feeling is bigger than what is real sometimes and that is not good. If you do not like this feeling, then why are you here?

Do you truly think that success comes through overcoming of failure? Do you feel that the more you hurdle through the better the outcome or the bigger the prize of you? (Or the price of you?) What is it that is holding you apart from the ease you are here to experience in this beautiful realm? Do you want have control over your life so much that you would rather trouble than peace?

The starving artist, the black and white poet. The dark knight. The depth in light. It is the mending of the mother and father wound that is here. Not the big picture. It is just the beginning truly not a voyage yet.

Why regret when things are final or complete?

Because you do not feel yet that there is more available to you.

If you recognized the abundance that life really has in store for you, you wouldn't stagnate here. You would recognise that in comparison to what you are offered you have little.

Life of grandeur blurred with emotional inconsistency is blue. Distrust for one's actions develops fast which leads to incompetence within no matter the physical or financial blueprint. Nothing matches with time. A blue experience of life where nothing is designed to elevate becomes a boring game. Just drop down to the ground again. How would you get your wings if flight isn't what you want?

Learn to live in simple terms if life isn't making sense. Then get back on the horse again. The answers will come for the seekers of truth. The doer and the creators don't have it easy but with work comes opportunity to expand and grow. It is always on the cards.

Generosity brings open spaces and gratitude of the All.

Now, if that doesn't feel good, you truly are lost…

"IF YOU RECOGNIZED THE ABUNDANCE THAT LIFE REALLY HAS IN STORE FOR YOU, YOU WOULDN'T STAGNATE HERE."

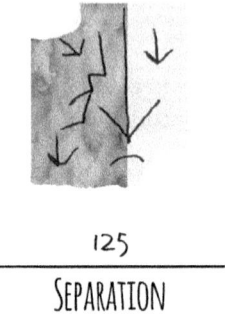

125
Separation

If you are a loss to your own self, you will be loss to all things. You can't find yourself in art you don't show or books you don't publish. You have to connect! Connect with us! Don't be afraid!

Bridge all gaps!

They are a waste of your time!

You'll never find yourself in people you don't approach because, the books you don't publish or the artworks you don't show. If you are there – in fear of your progress, or in fear of your opportunities, there is much to take to it's limit! If your dreams aren't lived they hang heavy on you. You can't openly live your simple human purpose if you keep yourself behind. You are human - a being that moves and communicates. Take it to the limit.

Separation is no fun for anybody even though it might feel creative somehow to be the tortured artist or the martyr. Let it go. Let your drawings, your sketches, your thoughts fly like chicks that have left their nest. They are yours but we too have them within us. They already exist within the collective understanding of all things. They are flying home when they are released by you. Back into us, back into you.

You have to be unleashed at least for fun if not for good. Let it be it! Let it burst, ring, feel itself born, fill the air, transcend all barriers and FLY!

These are your wings.

"BRIDGE ALL GAPS!"

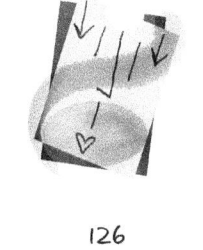

126
Trust

Nobody is hurt by you and nobody wants to hurt you. Creativity that is frowned on by another, jealousy, scheming, anger and violence – these are myths.

Nobody is scheming, nobody is bubbling underneath. There is no plot. It is all a game no one is playing. We have been fed fear of others for too long. We are all indeed open - we are not shadow lurking around the corners. Yes this world is sometimes strange with it's choices, but we see only a point in time, a perspective - not the full spiral, so yes it is easy to be confused. Don't believe in people's shadows. Become one with us. Trust.

Yes, trust us. Humour is welcome. Art is too. If you don't want to be seen or understood that is ok. We won't bother you, but whatever doesn't want to be seen or bothered often doesn't last. It disappears. Just as other humanoid species died out a long time ago. Hiding brings nothing good to a creature so big. So don't hide.

You don't have to be found or seen. You can just be you. But know that you are welcome. Understand what a welcome truly is.

"LET IT BE IT! LET IT BURST, RING, FEEL ITSELF BORN, FILL THE AIR, TRANSCEND ALL BARRIERS AND FLY!"

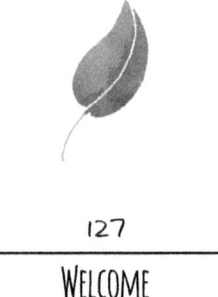

127
WELCOME

Welcome to nature, it is the force behind most things. Welcome is truth – the only truth of it's design. Nothing to fear, nothing to betray. All is listening, all is an open heart.

You are welcome. You perhaps do not feel welcome enough within yourself, which is common. If you cannot find your own self, your roots, your trees, your people - you aren't feeling welcome. So what is it that you want? What do you desire? We are listening.

Ask yourself that and answer quickly in as many ways as come to mind.

Is there a part of you that is looking to destroy and yet to please at the same time?

Are you a hurricane at work? Are you a burden? Or are you a tree that feeds all? Do you sing like the birds? Do you work like a bee? Do you mind your business like your parents did or do you find ways to be in everyone's lives? Do you love? Lead? Follow? Fold? Sleep?

Is it all just too much sometimes?

Do you maybe just desire an end and within that a beginning?

Be still….breathe….

"ALL IS LISTENING, ALL IS AN OPEN HEART."

Peace

Hello,

I'm Polina - creator of "Unleash the Beast". Perhaps we should get to know each other a little better now that you've been through this little rollercoaster. It is always nice to make new friends.

I haven't always been totally tuned in. Though I've always been sensitive, I started channelling and communicating with spirit consciously only in 2011, eventually understanding my psychic spectrum in 2015 after a period of shamanic initiations. My abilities weren't learned through anybody or anything – they were a by-product of need for life to truly feel as it should – as something inside me knew whatever I was living and whoever I became wasn't quite "it". I just knew I wasn't happy being the way I was. I asked to change, I also asked to help and heal others - and so it was given.

After discovering and confirming my psychic gifts, it was a long hard journey to get to the point where I could trust myself enough to communicate them fluently. Partially because of my cultural heritage being against it, partially because of my fear of myself, I was only able to tap into my ancestral memory and my true potential as a channel in my late 20s. It wasn't easy to see the full story but in the end it did become clear.

Through my life I have always wanted to learn more about this world – I knew who I was or what I had in my life somehow wasn't right, but no matter where I turned or who I turned to, nothing felt right till I personally learnt more about myself. It is through my learning of self that I started streaming knowledge and discovering more of the world both seen and unseen. My psychic abilities and my own personal joy and happiness peaked simultaneously as I learned more about me – who I truly was and what was possible for me personally. Through my own connection with myself I have learned much more about others and the world around me too. With every step towards oneness within me - spirit was kinder to me and more downloads were available. I was awakening.

Through discovering myself I became aware of the oneness of all things – which lead me to a life that was eventually a prefect fit.

As for most of us, fear of self is what stands in the way of our utter most joy and happiness. Working with this fear is what has brought me closure and eventually freedom when I learnt to understand it and through my work on myself and other people – connect it up to my blueprint as a piece that belonged, not a piece that worked against me anymore. My shadow became an invited guest not a foe, an understood component of my being here, which made it belong. My new connection to it made it work for me. I eventually saw the beauty and grace that was within it and it's place in the world.

As I was very afraid to be seen most of my life, my fear led me to many unconscious places until I started allowing it to speak and be heard without censorship. Without worry. Without grief. Without need. I just began talking and showing what I understood through the spirit realm un-phased by it's place, what it truly meant or whether it was right or wrong in someone else's eyes.

Through what I wasn't afraid of anymore new possibilities opened. Fearlessness realigned me to connect with all things – my birth right that was offcourse abandoned due to the way things are here on this planet for most people.

Through uncensored way of life, I have been able to create a well established digital presence as a psychic channel and astrologer. My business is successful due to my inability to fear myself anymore – which birthed the inability to lie. The ability to channel and perceive psychically without barriers depends on one's level of truth and understanding of all beings both seen and unseen as sacred – as well as oneself as full – one and sacred.

Thank you for connecting with my book. There are a few more coming.

Feel free to connect to me.

With love,

Polina

www.polinaoutkina.com

www.ingramcontent.com/pod-product-compliance
Lightning Source LLC
Chambersburg PA
CBHW070454100426
42743CB00010B/1611